The Bamboo Basket Handbook

英語訳付き

# 竹かごハンドブック

竹かごの素材、種類、選び方から、
編み方、メンテナンスまでわかる

誠文堂新光社

# はじめに
### Introduction

美しい手仕事から生まれる、日本の竹かご。その名は知られていても、ひとつのかごができるまでに、どれほどの手間や技、作り手の思いが込められているかは、これまであまり語られてきませんでした。そこで本書では、素材、技法、歴史などの"竹かごの基礎知識"だけでなく、人気作家が手作りしたいろいろな種類の竹かごを通じて、制作のこだわりや暮らしの中での使い方も紹介。竹かごの魅力を知りたいという方はもちろん、日本の生活文化を知りたい方の参考本としても、ご利用いただければと思います。

Japanese bamboo baskets are born from beautiful handmade craftwork. Even though these baskets are well known themselves, just how much technique, effort, and emotion is poured into each one is hardly ever spoken about. Therefore, this book aims to introduce not only "basic bamboo basket knowledge", such as materials, techniques, and history, but also through various types of baskets woven by many popular craftsmen and women, tips for making them, and how these baskets can be used in our everyday lives. A book not only for those who want to explore the world of Japanese bamboo basket making, but also for those who would like to get to know everyday Japanese culture.

# INDEX

## Chapter 1　ニッポンのいろいろなかご
【素材別編】

- 10　青物〜真竹〜
  - 12　茶碗かご
  - 14　味噌こしざる
  - 15　買い物かご
  - 16　米研ぎざる
  - 18　暮らしの中にある青物のかご
- 20　白物〜真竹〜
  - 22　鉄鉢
  - 24　八つ目小物入れ
  - 26　CARGO
  - 28　竹トレー
  - 30　パンかご
- 32　角物〜真竹〜
  - 34　竹BOX
  - 36　千筋三段重
  - 39　豆腐かご、おかべかご
- 40　"いろいろな竹"のかご
  - 42　すず竹の弁当箱
  - 44　篠竹の米研ぎざる
  - 46　根曲竹の蕎麦ざる
  - 47　オカメ笹の盛りかご

## Chapter 1  Various baskets in Japan

Sorted by material

- 10 **Aomono: Madake**
  - 12 Chawan basket
  - 14 Misokoshi zaru
  - 15 Shopping baskets
  - 16 Kometogi zaru
  - 18 Aomono baskets for everyday living

- 20 **Shiromono: Madake**
  - 22 Teppachi
  - 24 Yatsume accessory case
  - 26 CARGO
  - 28 Bamboo tray
  - 30 Bread basket

- 32 **Kakumono: Madake**
  - 34 Bamboo BOX
  - 36 3-tier sensuji
  - 39 Tofu basket & okabe basket

- 40 **Baskets made out of various bamboo**
  - 42 Suzutake bento lunchbox
  - 44 Sinodake bamboo kometogi zaru
  - 46 Nemagaridake soba zaru
  - 47 Okamezasa morikago

本書は小社より刊行された、『手づくりする竹のかごと器』
(2013年9月)と、『竹かご編みの技法書』(2014年8月)の
記事を一部抜粋し、英語訳をつけて再編集したものです。

INDEX

## Chapter 1  ニッポンのいろいろなかご
【アイテム別編】
- 48 お出かけするかご
  - 50 透かし網代編みのかごバッグ
  - 52 桝網代バッグ
  - 54 いろいろなかごバッグ
- 56 花籠
  - 57 花籠 宝珠
  - 58 花籠 白雲
  - 59 一輪挿し
  - 60 掛け花入れ
  - 61 茶籠など
- 62 ファッションアイテム

## Chapter 2  竹かごの基礎知識
- 68 日本の竹
- 70 日本の竹の特性
- 72 竹かごに使われる竹
- 75 竹かごの各部の名称
- 76 竹かごの歴史

## Chapter 3  竹材を用意する
- 80 竹を伐る
- 84 晒し竹を作る

## Chapter 4  竹ひご作り

## Chapter 5  編組（編み方）の種類

## Chapter 6  編み方
- 112 四つ目編み
- 124 六つ目編み

---

- 136 お手入れ方法
- 138 作家リスト
- 140 取扱店リスト

| | | |
|---|---|---|
| Chapter 1 | | Various baskets in Japan |
| | | Sorted by item |
| | 48 | Going out baskets |
| | | 50 Sukashi ajiro weave basket bag |
| | | 52 Masu ajiro bag |
| | | 54 Various basket bags |
| | 56 | Hanakago |
| | | 57 Hanakago hoju |
| | | 58 Hanakago shirakumo |
| | | 59 Ichirinzashi |
| | | 60 Kake hanaire |
| | | 61 Chakago and others |
| | 62 | Fashion accessories |
| Chapter 2 | | Bamboo basket basic knowledge |
| | | 68 Japanese bamboo |
| | | 70 Characteristics of japanese bamboo |
| | | 72 Bamboo used in bamboo baskets |
| | | 75 Naming each section of a bamboo basket |
| | | 76 History of bamboo baskets |
| Chapter 3 | | Preparing the bamboo |
| | | 80 Felling the bamboo |
| | | 84 Making bleached bamboo |
| Chapter 4 | | Making bamboo strips |
| Chapter 5 | | Types of weaves (weaving techniques) |
| Chapter 6 | | How to weave |
| | | 112 Yotsume weaves |
| | | 124 Mutsume weaves |
| | | 136 Care methods |
| | | 138 Craftsmen directory |
| | | 140 Retailer's List |

Chapter 1

# ニッポンの
# いろいろなかご

Various baskets in Japan

日本の暮らしの中に、
ずっと身近にあった竹のかご。
それぞれの地方で、
長く愛されてきた竹のかごたちを
まとめてみました。

Bamboo baskets are always close by
in Japanese life.
We've compiled a guide to
the long-beloved baskets from each region.

## 新潟県
Niigata Prefecture

佐渡／しちなりかご（真竹）
Sado / Shichinari kago (madake)

佐渡／味噌こしざる（真竹）
Sado / Misokoshi zaru (madake)

## 兵庫県
Hyogo Prefecture

深ざる（淡竹）
Fukazaru (hachiku)

## 大分県
Oita Prefecture

別府／鉄鉢（真竹）
Beppu / Teppachi (madake)

## 熊本県
Kumamoto Prefecture

日奈久／弁当箱（真竹）
Hinagu / Bento box (madake)

## 宮崎県
Miyazaki Prefecture

高千穂／カルイ（真竹）
Takachiho / Karui (madake)

### 岩手県
Iwate Prefecture

鳥越／おぼけ（すず竹）
Torigoe / Oboke (suzutake)

### 宮城県
Miyagi Prefecture

岩出山／米とぎざる（篠竹）
Iwadeyama / Kometogi zaru (shinodake)

大和／肥料かご（篠竹）
Taiwa / Hiryo kago (shinodake)

### 山梨県
Yamanashi Prefecture

蕎麦ざる（すず竹）
Soba zaru (suzutake)

### 茨城県
Ibaraki Prefecture

行方／ザップ（真竹）
Namegata / Zap (madake)

### 長野県
Nagano Prefecture

戸隠／蕎麦ざる（根曲竹）
Togakushi / Soba zaru (nemagaridake)

松本／蕎麦ざる（すず竹）
Matsumoto / Soba zaru (suzutake)

# 青物 〜真竹〜
あおもの
Aomono: Madake

日本の竹かごで最も多く使われるのは真竹です。伐採したままの竹を青竹と言うことから、青竹を素材としているものをかごの用語では「青物」と呼びます。昔から台所などで使われる暮らしの道具は、一般的に、自然のままの青竹で作られた青物でした。今、青物を作る継承者は数少なくなりましたが、昔ながらの生活道具をより美しい姿でよみがえらせている若手作家がいます。

The bamboo that is used the most in Japanese bamboo basket making is madake. Bamboo that is still in the state in which it was felled is called "aodake" (green bamboo), so things that are made from this bamboo are often called "aomono" in reference to the name of the material. From long ago, the everyday items used in places like the kitchen are generally aomono that are made from natural aodake. Nowadays, the number of successors to this craft has dropped, however there are younger craftsmen who are trying to breathe new life into these everyday tools by making them look more beautiful.

# 茶碗かご
Chawan basket

**勢司恵美 作**
By Emi Seishi

勢司恵美さんは、真竹の青物細工を継いでいる貴重な作り手のひとり。「昔から使われるかごを、昔からのやり方で作る」ことを大切にしながら、伝統技術を生かして、今の生活者が求める竹かご作りに日々挑んでいます。

　例えばそのひとつが、茶碗かご。シンプルですが、縦にすっと広がるシルエットが特徴的です。さらに縁部分のきれいな斜めのラインが、かごの美しさをより印象深いものにしています。

　「縁は青竹の表皮を削ってなめらかにする、磨きという技法で仕上げています。縁は手に触れるところですから、手触りが良い方が自然と手を出しやすくなるのではと考えました」と勢司さん。

　日々使われる日用品だからこそ、使いたいと思われる"美しい道具"に仕上げたい。そんな思いが込もっている逸品です。

Emi Seishi is one of these precious successors who makes aomono out of madake bamboo. By making a point of creating traditionally used baskets in the way that they were traditionally made, she is able to make the most of traditional techniques, and challenges herself to make baskets that are needed by the people of today.

One of these baskets is the chawan basket. Though it's a simple basket, its straight upwards silhouette is its main characteristic. The slanted lines at the rim area also help to give this basket an even more impressive beauty.

"The rim is finished with a technique known as "migaki" where the surface of the aodake is torn off to create a smoother feel. Since the rim is where the hands tend to come into contact with the basket, it's thought that by making it feel nicer, people will be more likely to use it," says Seishi.

"As the basket is something that is used everyday, I wanted to finish it into a "beautiful tool", that people will actually want to use. This is a beauty of a basket that is packed full of such feelings.

茶碗かごの縁。勢司さんの仕上げへのこだわりが伝わってくる、斜めにそろった美しいライン。

The rim of the chawan basket. The beautiful diagonal lines are indicative of Seishi's impeccable finishes.

# 味噌こしざる

Misokoshi zaru

勢司恵美 作
By Emi Seishi

菊底編みで底を編んでいるところ。

The base is woven with a kiku base weave.

胴部分はござ目編みで編みあげていく。

The trunk is woven upwards with a gozame weave.

　「味噌こしざる」は、その名の通り、味噌汁を作るとき味噌をこして大豆などの細片を除くための道具。持ち手がある味噌こしざるもありますが、勢司さんの作品の中で「使い勝手が良い」と幅広い層に好まれているのが、持ち手のないシンプルで小さなタイプです。

　「今の時代、味噌をこすために使う人はあまりいなくなりました。購入してくださる方も私自身も、プチトマトのような小ぶりな野菜を洗うときなどに便利に使っています」。

As the name suggests, this is a tool for straining out bits of soy beans etc. when making miso soup. Though there are misokoshi zaru with handles, Seishi's works are well liked on a range of levels for their "ease-of-use" and this is a small and simple handleless design.
"It seems that nowadays nobody uses the misokoshi zaru for straining miso anymore. However I, and many of my customers, find it useful in the washing of small vegetables like cherry tomatoes."

# 買い物かご
Shopping baskets

### 勢司恵美 作
By Emi Seishi

勢司さんが制作した買い物かごの手付き部分。針金や木工ボンドは使わずに、自分で作った竹釘を使っている。

A hand crafted part of Seishi's shopping basket. Here she is using bamboo hooks that she made herself, rather than wire hooks or wood glue.

　奥は、勢司さんがいつも使っている自作の買い物かご。そして手前は、作ったばかりの買い物かごで、まだ青々しています。
　使うほどに青色から飴色に変化していく、それが青物を使う魅力だという人は少なくありません。

The basket further back is the shopping basket that Seishi made and uses herself. And the one at the front is a basket that she just made, and still has its vivid green colouring.
The colour turns from green to amber with prolonged use, which many people say is one of the attractive parts of owning aodake goods.

# 米研ぎざる

Kometogi zaru

### 内原聖次 作
By Seiji Uchihara

米が詰まるのを避けるため、内側の段差をなくすなど随所に工夫が見られる。

To prevent the rice getting stuck in cracks, Uchihara can be seen using tricks, such as closing the gaps between levels on the inside of the zaru, all over the place.

昔の日本では、お米を研ぐときに竹などの自然素材で編まれた「米研ぎざる」という道具を使っていました。1960年代になると、ステンレスやプラスチックのざるが代わって使われるようになりましたが、今、竹で作られた米研ぎざるが再評価されています。

　中でも人気なのが、竹工芸作家・内原聖次さんの作品です。そもそも、竹で作られた米研ぎざるには、「竹の面で米がほどよくこすれるので、力強く研がなくてもいい」というメリットがあります。それに加えて内原さんの米研ぎざるには、「縁が外側にあるので、縁に米が詰まりにくい」という、従来品にはない機能性が備わっています。

　けれど、内原さんの米研ぎざるの何よりの魅力は、使い心地。竹と米のすれる音がなんとも気持ち良いのです。

In the past, Japanese people used to polish rice in utensils woven from natural materials such as bamboo and known as "kometogi zaru". Though plastic and stainless steel utensils replaced them in the 1960's, kometogi zaru are now starting to make a comeback.

This is a popular product, even for Seiji Uchihara's range. Bamboo kometogi zaru originally had the merit of "rubbing the rice up somewhat with their bamboo surface, meaning that less effort had to be put into the polishing". On top of that, the rim of Uchihara's kometogi zaru has an extra feature not seen until now; a rim attached to the outside, meaning that it's difficult for rice to get stuck in it.

However, the most attractive thing about Uchihara's kometogi zaru is how good it feels to use. The sound of bamboo and rice rubbing together is music to the ears.

[ Chapter 1 ]

竹皮の表皮を削っている内原さん。磨きの技法を用いて、ひごを作っていく。米研ぎざるでは長いひごを使うので、4m以上の真竹が必要になるという。

Uchihara shaving the surface of some bamboo bark. He's making some bamboo strips using his migaki techniques. As kometogi zaru require longer strips, it appears that madake longer than 4m is necessary.

# 暮らしの中にある青物のかご

Aomono baskets for everyday living

## 内原聖次 作
By Seiji Uchihara

内原聖次さんが制作した青物のかごたち。作ったばかりのときは青々としていた青物の竹かごは、日々使ううちに、写真のような飴色になります。
(左から)片口ざる、六つ目編みの盛りかご、バンクーラー。片口ざるは、口が付いたざるのことで、洗った米を炊飯器に移すときなどに便利ですが、内原さんは自分で焙煎したコーヒー豆を容器に移すときによく使うそうです。パンクーラーは、料理教室を開く妻の由季さんのために作ったもの。金物のパンクーラーの形状を参考に、網目を大きくして足をつけ、通気性を高める工夫がほどこされています。

These are aomono baskets created by Seiji Uchihara. The vivid greens of freshly made baskets transform into an amber color over time and with daily use.
(From left) A lipped kataguchi zaru, a mutusme weave morikago, and a cooling rack. As the katakuchi zaru has a lip, it's very useful for things such as transferring rice to the rice cooker, however Uchihara uses it to store and transport his home-roasted coffee beans. The cooling rack is something he made for his wife, Yuki, who teaches cookery classes. Using the shape of a metal cooling rack as a guide, he made the stitches bigger and gave it stands to improve ventilation.

[ Chapter 1 ]

# 白物 〜真竹〜
### Shiromono: Madake

油抜きの下処理をした竹を、晒し竹または白竹と言います。どちらも竹の植物学的な名前ではなく、竹かご用語です。青竹で作る青物に対し、晒し竹で作るかごは「白物」と呼ばれます。白物で、独特の作風を確立してきた大分県の別府では、若手作家がそれぞれにデザイン性の高い作品を作っています。

After bamboo has been prepared by extracting the oil, it becomes known as bleached bamboo (sarashidake) or shiratake. Neither of these names is scientific, both are purely bamboo basket terms. As products made from aodake are called "aomono", products made from bleached bamboo are called "shiromono". The young craftsmen of Beppu in Oita Prefecture, which has established its own unique style, continue to produce particularly well-designed work.

# 鉄鉢
Teppachi

**児玉美重 作**
By Mie Kodama

児玉さんはフルーツやお菓子を入れる盛りかごとして使っている。

Kodama uses the teppachi as a morikago to serve fruit and sweets.

鉄鉢の底部分を編んでいる児玉さん。

Kodama weaves the base of the teppachi.

お坊さんが托鉢するときの鉄の鉢に見立てたことから、この名がついた「鉄鉢」。人間国宝の故人・生野祥雲齋が考案した、別府竹工芸伝統の盛りかごです。

　昭和の時代、日本の食卓ではミカンを入れる盛りかごとしてよく見かけたものですが、今、竹細工ならではの透かした編み目の美しさに、あらためて魅了される人は少なくありません。別府で竹工芸を学び、現在は隣接した城下町・杵築市で制作活動を行っている竹工芸作家の児玉美重さんも、そのひとりです。

　鉄鉢のサイズは規格化され、2枚の輪弧編みを重ねて編むという技法も継承されていますが、「目の詰め方によるラインをどう変えたか」「底の編み方を何にしたのか」など、作り手の個性を発見できるのも見どころです。

　「私が底編みに選んだのは麻の葉編みです。ですが、麻の葉編みの正六角形では和の雰囲気が強くなると感じたので、少しアレンジを加えて縦長にしてみました」と話す児玉さんの鉄鉢には、伝統美を今の暮らしにうまくなじませたセンスと技が凝縮されています。

So named for the resemblence to the traditional metal bowls used by Buddhist monks when asking for money. This is a traditional Beppu bamboo craft morikago designed by the now-deceased national treasure Ikuno Shounsai.
During the Showa period it was common to see baskets of mikan oranges on the table, but even now, people are starting to once again notice the attractiveness of the sukashi gapped-weave that's typical of traditional bamboo work. One of these people is Mie Kodama, a student of traditional Beppu bamboo work and a craftswoman in the adjoining castle town of Kitsuki.
Though the size of the teppachi is standardized and the rinko weave, where 2 sets of weave are put on top of each other, passed down, there are still lots of places where you can see the maker's individual personality shine through, such as where they've thought about changing the lines to catch the eye, or which weave they've chosen for the base.
"I chose the asanoha weave for the base. However, as I felt that the perfect hexagonal shapes of the asanoha weave made my basket feel a bit too Japanese, I adjusted it a little to make them more oblong shaped," says Kodama about her teppachi, which has used sense and technique to combine traditional beauty with something that blends seamlessly into everyday life.

# 八つ目小物入れ
Yatsume accessory case

**児玉美重 作**
By Mie Kodama

編み目が八角形であることから「八つ目編み」と呼ばれる編み方です。八角形の間には小さな四角形もあって、八角と四角の美しいコラボレーションが印象的です。

洋風の雰囲気がする八つ目編みは、"見せるかご"によく使われます。児玉さんのように、いろどりのきれいな器を収納すれば、ちょっとしたインテリアにもなります。

また、四角いかごは使い勝手がいいので、テーブルの上にある雑然とある小物をまとめるのにも便利です。

This weave is called the "yatsume weave" because of the octagonal stitches that it forms. In between these octagons, little squares can be found, forming an impressive collaboration of shapes.

The yatsume weave, which has a bit of a Western feel to it, is often used in display baskets. If you do like what Kodama has done and fill it with colour, it also adds to the interior design of your room.

Square baskets are very convenient and are useful for storing any accessories and clutter found on places like the table.

縁は、流し巻きという巻き方。籐が持つシンプルだけれどモダンな雰囲気が、八つ目編みの洋の雰囲気とうまく調和している。

The rim is made in a nagashimaki style. The simple yet modern feeling of the cane harmonizes perfectly with the Western feel of the basket.

児玉さんは、縁側でティータイムを過ごすときのお茶セット入れとして活用。

Kodama makes use of this basket by storing her tea set in it.

# CARGO
CARGO

清水貴之 作
By Takayuki Shimizu

CARGOにお風呂セットを入れ、別府の町を歩く清水さん。温泉地として知られる別府には公共温泉が点在しており、町の人たちが毎日のように利用している。

Shimizu walks through the streets of Beppu with his bath set in his CARGO. There are lots of little communal hot springs dotted around Beppu, which is known as a hot spring resort, and which are used by the people on a daily basis.

竹工芸作家・清水貴之さんのCARGOは、「若い世代にも購入しやすい価格帯の竹かごを作りたい」という顧客志向がきっかけでした。

　手間がかかることから、価格を押し上げる要因になっていた縁の仕上げ方に着目し、縁を止めずかごの上でまとめるデザインを考案。結果、「竹かごは民芸的」という固定概念をくつがえした"おしゃれ感"のある竹かごに仕上がっています。

　「CARGOは縁がない分、強度に弱点があります。強度を保ちつつ、重ねて結べるほどの柔軟性を得るという課題をクリアするのに苦労しました」と振り返る清水さんがたどり着いたのは、ひごを薄く剥ぐ「2枚剥ぎ」という技法。

　例えば厚さ0.5mmと0.25mmのひごでは、0.5mmの方が強度はあります。柔軟性はと言えば、0.25mmの方が勝ります。そこで清水さんは、0.25mmのひごを2枚重ねてみることに。強度は増し、薄く柔らかいから2枚重ねても容易に曲げやすい、というわけです。

　新ジャンルの竹かごは、確かな伝統の技と、作家の試行錯誤から生まれました。

The reason that bamboo craftsman Takayuki Shimizu produced this basket was because he wanted to make something "in the price range of even younger customers." Through much effort, he managed to come up with a design that pushed costs down by focusing on the rim and making it so that the baskets could stack on top of each other. As a result, he managed to come up with some fashionable baskets that still managed to adhere to the concept that "bamboo baskets are folk craft".

"As CARGO have no rims, their strength is their weak point. I had to work hard to solve the problem of preserving the strength while obtaining the flexibility to build upon and connect the strips," says Shimizu as he reflects on the technique he finally developed to do this; "nimaihagi (two-strip tearing)", where the strips are torn very thinly. To give an example, strips that are 0.5mm thick are stronger than those that are 0.25mm thick. However, when Shimizu tried layering 2 of the weaker strips together, he found that their strength increased and as they were thin and flexible, they were also easy to bend.

It seems that a new genre of bamboo baskets has been born out of established traditional technique and the trial and error of a craftsman.

# 竹トレー
Bamboo tray

**清水貴之 作**
By Takayuki Shimizu

CARGOシリーズの
ワインかご。
A wine basket from
the CARGO series.

竹の編み目を活かし
た照明。
Lighting that makes
use of the weave of the
bamboo.

取引先のショップから「洋風で、端がちょっと立っているトレーを作れないか」と相談を受けた清水さん。どちらも難題ですが、ちょっと立てるという課題は「火曲げ」という技法でクリア。もうひとつの洋風という課題は、シンプルさの中にヒントがあるのではないかと、清水さんは考えました。

　「別府では、縁を止める際に籐を利用することが多いのですが、竹だけで仕上げればシンプルになり、むしろ洋風に近づくのではないかと思いました」

　それは、「足すのではなく、引いていくと、そこに美がある」という発想。そして、籐の代わりに竹で作られた釘（竹釘）を使い、四つ目編みのモダンな印象をそのまま活かした、究極にシンプルなトレーが完成しました。

Upon being asked by a client if he could make a "Western-style bamboo tray with ends that stick up", Shimizu rose to this difficult challenge by employing a "himage" technique to the ends and giving a slight accent to the simple design.
"In Beppu there are lots of cases where people use cane to rim the edges, but by finishing the edges simply with plain old bamboo, the tray achieves a simpler and more Western-style look."
This is the very idea that "beauty is drawn out rather than added on to something". Furthermore, instead of cane nails, Shimizu has opted for those made from bamboo, has given the basket a modern impression by using the yotsume weave, and has finally created the ultimate in simple trays.

清水さんの住まいの台所。

The kitchen in Shimizu's home.

# パンかご
Bread Basket

**大谷健一 作**
By Kenichi Otani

ゆるやかなカーブで無理なく立ち上げた角。
A gentle curve with natural corners.

「昔の暮らしの道具には、大きさにも意味がありました。例えば膳は、人が持つときの肩幅を考えて運びやすい寸法になったそうです。また箸は、手を開いたときの親指と人差し指の長さがもとになっているんです」

そう教えてくれた竹工芸作家の大谷健一さんは、自らの竹かご作りで「何を入れるための"かご"か」をとても大切に考えています。

このパンかごは、短めのバゲットを入れることを想像して作ったもの。日本的な印象を抱かれがちな竹かごですが、パンを入れる器のように、洋風の使い方をする人は意外に多いのです。

編み方は、二本とびござ目編み。ござ目編みは強度があることから、昔から「ざる」などの暮らしの道具によく使われてきました。2本、3本と、とばす数が増えるほどに目が大きくなり、雰囲気も違ってきますが、大谷さんは、「2本とばしは絶妙に良い加減で、清潔感のある表情が私は大好きです」と評しています。

大谷さんの熟練の技が成した品のある美しい盛りかごは、パンかごとしてだけでなく、「おもてなしの器」として好まれているのもうなずけます。

"For traditional tools there was a meaning to the size. For example, small zen dining tables were built to the width of a person's shoulders to make it easy to carry, and chopsticks were made based on the length of the thumb and forefinger of an open hand," says bamboo craftsman Otani, who always seriously thinks about what he wants to put inside a basket before making it.

He made this bread basket with the image of a small baguette in mind. Though bamboo baskets tend to leave a very Japanese impression, there is a surprising amount of people who use these baskets for a more Western-style purpose such as storing bread.

The weave is a nihontobi gozame weave. Gozame weaves are quite strong, so have often been used for items such as zaru plates. The larger the number of missed strips, such as in nihontobi (2 missed strips), or sanbontobi (3 missed strips), the larger the gaps in the stitching, giving each basket its own individual feel. Otani has a preference for nihontobi, saying that "two is the perfect number and I love the clean expression of the stitching".

The beautiful morikago baskets made with Otani's skillful techniques are not only loved as bread baskets, but can also be used for entertaining guests.

# 角物 ～真竹～
## Kakumono: Madake

四角い竹かごを「角物」と言います。九州には、角物の作り手は一時期たくさんいたそうですが、今では数えるばかりです。ここでは、まったく違うスタイルで、伝統を継いでいる角物の作り手の竹かごを紹介します。

Rectangular bamboo baskets called "kakumono". There used to be many makers of these kakumono in Kyushu, but nowadays the number has dwindled considerably. Here we will introduce a number of kakumono made with traditional techniques and that have their own individual twists.

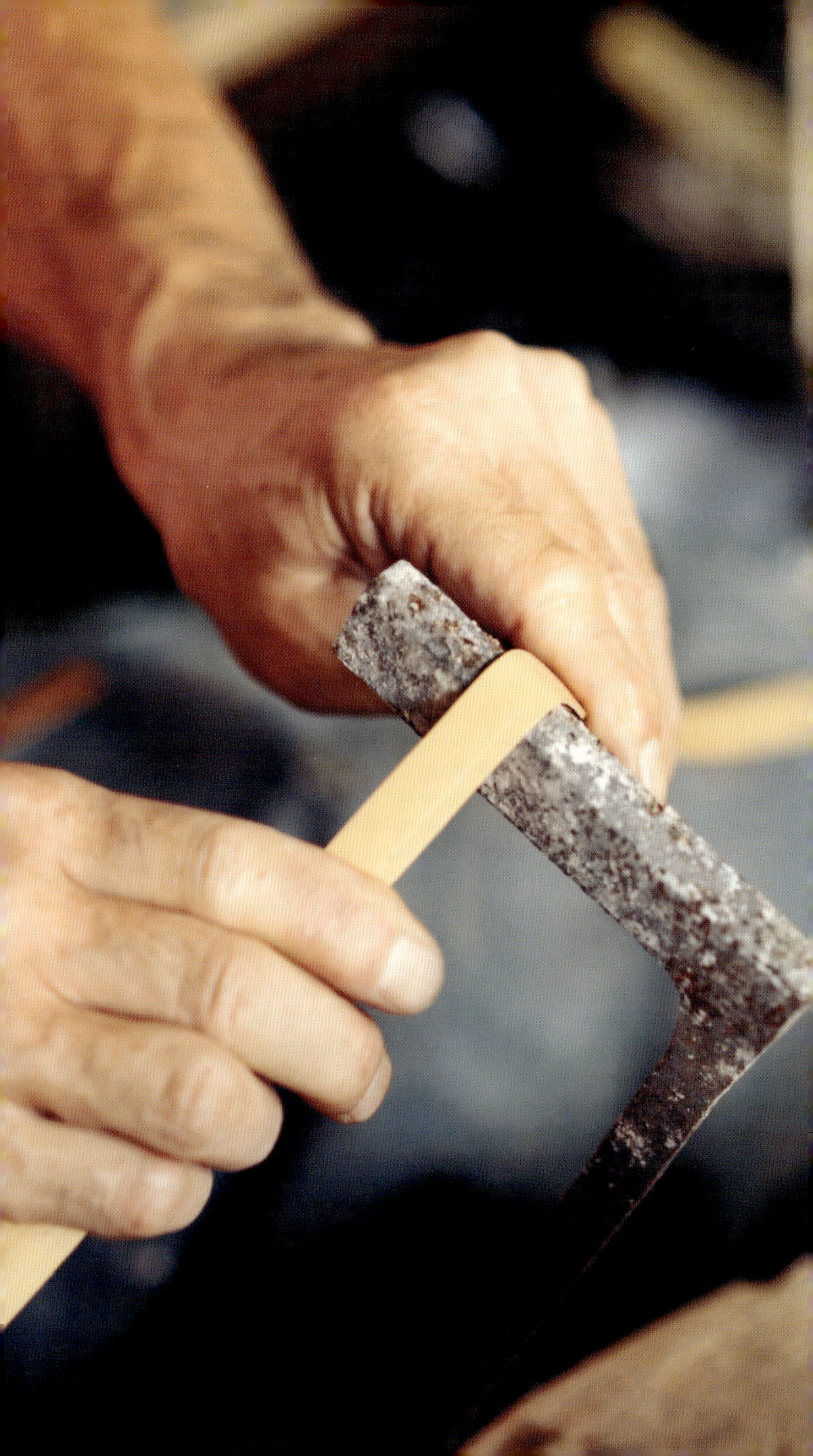

# 竹BOX
Bamboo BOX

**岩田淳子 作**
By Junko Iwata

竹BOXのサイズは21㎝×21㎝。岩田さんはピクニックバスケットとしても活用している。

The size of the Bamboo BOX is 21cm x 21cm. Iwata often uses hers as a picnic basket.

「豆腐かご」はその名の通り、豆腐を運ぶための道具。太めのひごで編まれるかごは、北欧のバスケットにも似ていて、最近では収納かごとして使う人も増えています。竹工芸作家の岩田淳子さんもまた、美しい晒し竹で作られた豆腐かごに魅了されたひとり。そして、昔から使われてきた豆腐かごの良さを引き継ぎつつ、今の暮らしに合うアレンジを加えた角物のかご「竹BOX」を考案しました。

　「豆腐を運ぶという本来の使い方からすれば、底の編み目は荒くてもいいのですが、今は収納が主な用途。ならば、底は緻密にできていた方が使いやすいと思いました」

　きっちりていねいに、心を込めて手作りされる岩田さんの竹BOXは、角物好きのみならず、幅広い層に愛用されています。

As the name suggests a "tofu basket" is used to carry tofu. Baskets woven with wider strips resemble baskets from northern Europe, and have started to be used increasingly as storage baskets.Bamboo craftswoman Junko Iwata is one person attracted to gorgeous tofu baskets made with bleached bamboo, and weaves baskets that not only preserve the quality of those that were made in the past, but also cater to the needs of modern living, which she has called "Bamboo BOX".

"These baskets were used to carry tofu in the past, so it didn't matter if the basket was made quite roughly, but now as they're being utilized more and more for storage, I think they're easier to use if the stitches are more precise."

Iwata's carefully and tightly woven handmade Bamboo BOX is not only liked by kakumono lovers, but by all kinds of people.

竹CUBEのサイズは15㎝×15㎝。ちょっとした小物を入れるのに便利だし、一人分のお弁当入れとしても使いやすい。

The size of the Bamboo CUBE is 15cm x 15cm. It's great for storing accessories and other small items, or even to store a bento lunch for one.

# 千筋三段重

3-tier sensuji

**桑原哲次郎 作**
By Tetsujiro Kuwabara

熊本県の日奈久温泉に竹細工が始まったのは明治時代。約100年、技は継承され、現在は桑原哲次郎さんが、伝統の「千筋三段重」を手作りしています。三段のお重にはそれぞれ、おかず、おにぎり、果物を入れることを想定しています。昔の日本は3世代同居の家が多かったので、お弁当持参で出かけるときには、この三段重の大きさがちょうど良かったのです。そうした使われ方がなくなった今では、たたずまいの優美さから、化粧箱や小物入れなどに愛用されています。

　千筋とは、筋が千本もあるような細かい縞模様のこと。細いひごを「ござ目編み」で編み、細かい縞模様の編地を作ります。桑原さんの手による編地は、機織りで織られた布のような美しさ。伝統の職人技は、確かに継がれています。

Bamboo crafting started at the Hinagu hot springs in Kumamoto Prefecture during the Meiji period. For approximately 100 years, these skills have been passed down, and Tetsujiro Kuwabara currently hand-makes the traditional "3-tier sensuji" bento box. Each tier is designed to carry a separate type of dish, side dishes, onigiri rice, balls, and fruit. In the past in Japan, it was very common for families to live together in 3 generations, so the size of this 3-tier bento box was perfect for the amount of food needed when eating out. Now the box is needed less for such things, it has started to become used more for the storage of make-up and accessories due to its elegant shape. The word "sensuji" means "thousand strips", which refers to the fact that the box looks to have a fine striped pattern. Thin bamboo strips are woven into a gozame weave to make this box, generating this effect. The boxes woven by Kuwabara's hands are as beautiful as fabric woven in a loom, proving that the old techniques continue to live on within him.

[ Chapter 1 ]

縞模様の編地を作っているところ。
Making the finely detailed weave.

竹ひごに穴をあける道具も手作り。
The tool used to make holes in the bamboo strips is also handmade.

# 角物の作り方
How to make kakumono

　角物の作り方は、一般的な竹かごの作り方とは異なり、数種類のひごを使い、パーツを組み合わせるように編んでいきます。

The way to make kakumono differs from the normal way of making bamboo baskets, using many different types of bamboo strips, and having each part woven so that they can be joined together.

例えば豆腐かごには、15種類のひごが使われている。

15 types of bamboo strips are used in this tofu basket for example.

角物では直角に曲がったひごを使う。直角のひごは火曲げという技法で作る。熱をあてて竹を曲げていくのだが、早く強くやれば折れてしまうので曲げる加減が難しい。

Kakumono use bamboo strips that are bent at right-angles. The strips are made by a technique called "himage". This is achieved by applying heat to the strips and bending them, however if done too quickly and forcefully there is a risk of folding them, so it's hard to get it just right.

四つ目いかだ底編みという編み方で、底を編んでいる岩田さん。

Iwata weaves the base using a yotsume ikada base weave.

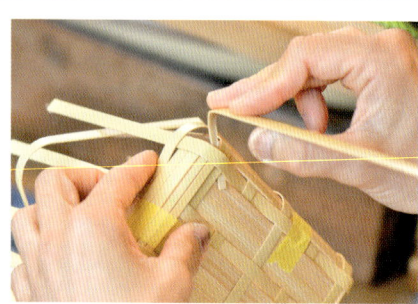

胴部分を編んでいるところ。

Weaving the trunk.

# 豆腐かご
Tofu basket

### 内原聖次 作
By Seiji Uchihara

青竹に磨きという技法をほどこした竹ひごで作った豆腐かご。昔からの豆腐かごに比べてスタイリッシュな表情。サンドイッチを入れてピクニックに出かけたり、屋外でのパーティーでも活躍しています。

This is a tofu basket that is made of aodake strips that have had a technique called "migaki" (polishing) applied to them. Compared to traditional tofu baskets, it's much more stylish. Great for carrying sandwiches to picnics, or for taking things to parties.

# おかべかご
Okabe basket

撮影協力:世界のかご カゴアミドリ
Photo: Sekai no Kago Kagoamidori

豆腐のことを鹿児島弁で「おかべ」ということから、豆腐かごのことを鹿児島では「おかべかご」と言います。鹿児島在住の作り手による、写真のおかべかごは、お弁当用に二段重ねにしたものです。

As tofu is called "okabe" in Kagoshima, tofu baskets are referred to as "okabe baskets" there. The okabe basket in the photograph has been made into a 2-tier basket for bento lunches by a Kagoshima-based maker.

## "いろいろな竹"のかご
Baskets made out of various bamboo

真竹の他にも、素材として使われている竹がいろいろあります。主なものが、東北や甲信越地方で見られる、すず竹、根曲竹、篠竹など。熟練の作り手の技で、それぞれの素材の特性を活かした、素敵なかごが作られています。

There are many different types of bamboo that are used in bamboo basket making aside from madake. Some main types that you can see in the Tohoku and Koshinetsu regions of Japan are suzutake, nemagaridake, and shinodake, etc. The characteristics of each type are utilized by each maker's skillful techniques to create fantastic baskets.

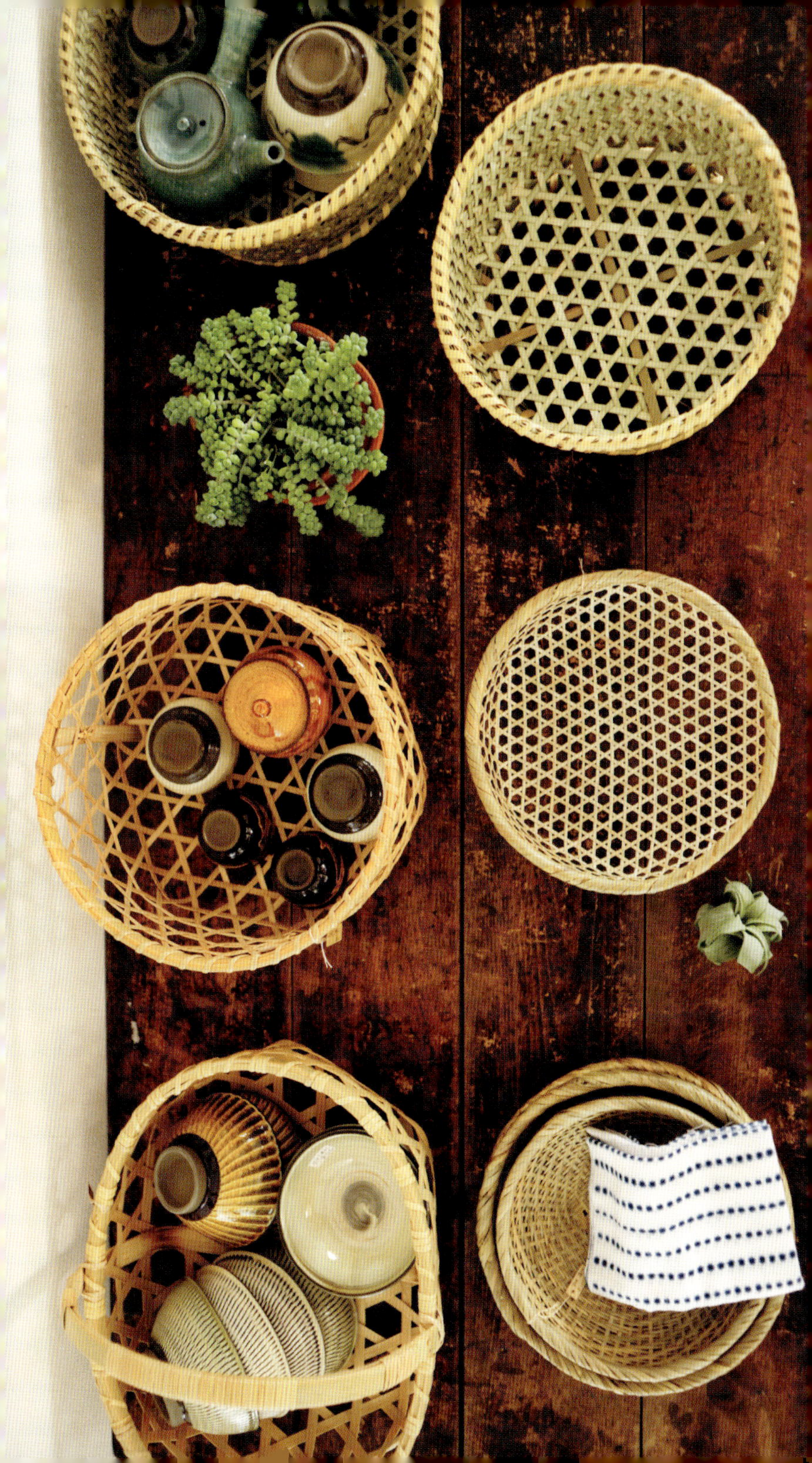

# すず竹の弁当箱
Suzutake bento lunchbox

### 柴田恵 作
By Megumi Shibata

弁当箱。作りたては竹の緑色をしている。すず竹のかごは通気性がいいので、蒸れにくい。

A bento lunchbox. It has a green finish from the colour of the bamboo. As suzutake is so breathable, it makes it hard for mould to develop.

岩手県一戸町鳥越地区は「鳥越のすず竹細工」の名で知られる、かごの産地。材料になるのは、地元で自生する、すず竹です。東北の厳しい風雪に鍛えられて育つすず竹はしなやかで、すず竹細工のかごは、指で押すと跳ね返してくる弾力性があるのが特徴です。

　その特性を最大限に活かし、新たな作品を発信し続けているのが竹工芸作家の柴田恵さんです。写真の重ねられたかごは、「小文庫」「お弁当箱」「名刺入れ」。柴田さんの繊細な手仕事で編まれるかごたちは美しく、上品なたたずまい。使い込むほどに独特の風合いが出てくるのが、日々使う楽しみでもあります。

The area of Torigoe in the city of Ichinohe in Iwate Prefecture is known from the name "Torigoe Suzutake crafts" and is an area that produces bamboo baskets. These baskets use the suzutake that grows in the local area. Suzutake that grows and endures in the harsh, snowy, and windy climate of Tohoku has a glaze and an elasticity so great that it will spring back when pushed with a finger.

One of those utilizing these traits and promoting new products is craftswoman Megumi Shibata. The works piled in the photo are a "storage box", "bento lunchbox", and a "business card holder". Shibata's finely hand-woven baskets are beautiful with an elegant shape. Their particular feel is so nice that you could end up wanting to use these baskets every day.

椀かごをアレンジして作ったマガジンラック。椀かごをスタイリッシュなマガジンラックに変身させてしまうなんて、その想像力がすごい。

This is a magazine rack made by adjusting the wan basket design. It must have taken a lot of imagination to be able to turn a wan basket into such a stylish magazine rack.

# 篠竹の米研ぎざる

Shinodake bamboo kometogi zaru

撮影協力:大崎市竹工芸館
Photo: Osaki Bamboo Crafts Hall

宮城県大崎市内の旧・岩出山は、「岩出山の篠竹細工」で知られるところ。山野に自生する篠竹を使った竹かご作りは、江戸時代、武士の内職として始まりました。明治になると農閑期の女性の内職として受け継がれましたが、他のかごの産地がそうであるように、1960年代になるとプラスチック製品におされ、激減してしまいます。

　けれど今、岩出山の篠竹細工の人気が再燃。皮の部分を内側に使った米研ぎざるは、水切れがとてもいいのです。

　米研ぎざるが知られていますが、岩出山の篠竹細工で「伝統ざる」と呼ばれるのが、写真の8つのざる。米研ぎによく使われるのは小さなサイズで、大きいものは農具や配達用などの働く道具として使われていたそうです。

The name of the town of Iwadeyama, which is now located within Osaki City, Miyagi Prefecture, is known through "Iwadeyama Shinodake crafts". The creation of baskets made from the shinodake bamboo that grows in the mountains was a side job for samurai during the Edo period, and was also taken up by women in the Meiji period when there was little work to do on the farms, but just like many other basket weaving regions, work dried up as demand dropped in favour of plastic products in the 1960's. However, the popularity of Iwadeyama shinodake goods is now back on the rise, and the kometogi zaru that have the bark part of the bamboo on the inside are great for draining.

Though kometogi zaru are well known, Iwadeyama shinodake works known as "dentou zaru" (traditional zaru) are made up of the 8 zaru shown in the photograph. The small zaru are often used for polishing rice, while the larger zaru are often used as tools in farming, and delivery and distribution.

仕上がったばかりの米研ぎざる。硬さや厚さの異なる数種類のひごを材料に、しっかりと作られている。

A newly finished kometogi zaru. It's made well with bamboo strips of differing hardness and thickness and made from several kinds of bamboo.

# 根曲竹の蕎麦ざる
## Nemagaridake soba zaru

井上栄一 作
By Eiichi Inoue

根曲竹。右が2、3年物。左が3カ月物。主として2、3年物を使うが、縁を巻くところはやわらかい3カ月物を使うなど、4種類のひごを使い分けて蕎麦ざるは作られる。

Nemagaridake. On the right is nemagaridake that is 2-3 months old. That on the left is 3 months old. 2-3 month old bamboo is used mainly, but the 3 month old nemagaridake is supple and can be used wrapped around the rim, making for a soba zaru that's made up of 4 different kinds of bamboo strips.

　根曲竹のかごの産地では、青森県の弘前と長野県の戸隠が知られています。りんごの生産量日本一の弘前では、りんごを収穫するときに使う「りんごかご」が作られてきました。一方の戸隠は、日本三大蕎麦のひとつと言われる戸隠蕎麦が有名で、根曲竹で作られた「蕎麦ざる」が活躍しています。

　根曲竹は丈夫で粘りがあります。押しても戻ってくる強さが特徴であり良さでもあります。根曲竹の強さを生かして作られる蕎麦ざるは、とても丈夫。時にはフルーツを盛ったりと、ひとつの蕎麦ざるで、いろいろな使い方を楽しむこともできます。

Hirosaki in Aomori Prefecture and Togakushi in Nagano Prefecture are known as places where nemagaridake bamboo baskets are produced. Hirosaki, which can also boast the fact that it produces the most apples in all of Japan, has always made "apple baskets" to use in harvesting the apples. On the other hand, Togakushi is one of the big 3 soba noodle producers in Japan, producing famous Togakushi soba noodles, and where nemagaridake bamboo is used to make soba zaru plates.

Nemagaridake bamboo is robust and has a certain tenacity to it. When pressed, it is strong enough to return to its original shape among other good points. Soba zaru that make use of the strength of nemagaridake are very robust. They can be used for displaying fruit, or even just as normal soba noodle zaru plates among other things.

# オカメ笹の盛りかご

Okamezasa morikago

### 新井ラク 作
By Raku Arai

40年、50年と長持ちする丈夫な暮らしの道具。写真は、約100年前に作られたという盛りかごで、現役で活躍しているという。

These okamezasa baskets are very robust and can be used for 40-50 years. The photograph shows a morikago that was made around 100 years ago and is still in use today.

　高さ1mほどしかないオカメ笹は、名前は「笹」でも竹類の1種。埼玉県や群馬県の一部地方では昔から、かご作りの材料として利用されてきました。
　水をあげない冬場に採取し、葉はきれいに取り、かご編みに使うのは幹の部分。天日干ししたりせずそのまま使うので、仕上がったばかりのかごは青々としています。みかんを入れる「みかんかご」の愛称で親しまれてきましたが、通気性がいいので、写真のように蒸し物の盛り付けにも利用できます。幹の表面はつるんとしているので水をよくはじくことから、野菜を洗う台所用のざるとして使う人もいるそうです。

Okamezasa, which only grows to a height of 1m, may have the name "zasa" (bamboo grass), but it is actually a type of bamboo, and has been used in the making of bamboo baskets in some parts of Saitama and Gunma Prefecture from long ago.

If harvested in winter without watering, the leaves can be taken away cleanly and the trunk used in weaving. It's used as-is, without drying it in the sun, giving newly finished baskets a beautiful vivid green colour. Though these baskets have become well used as baskets for mikan oranges, earning the nickname "mikan baskets", as they're so breathable, they're also great for serving steamed foods like in the photograph. As the trunk of the bamboo is so smooth, zaru that use okamezasa are good at repelling water and are sometimes used in the kitchen when washing vegetables.

## お出かけするかご
### Going out baskets

昔からの暮らしの道具だけでなく、かごバッグも日常のアイテムとして親しまれています。素材に関わらず「お出かけするかご」というくくりで、いろいろな竹かごを集めてみました。

Not only are these baskets traditional tools for living, basket bags have stayed close to us as an everyday item. Many baskets are grouped into this "going out bag" bamboo bracket, without it mattering about the material that they're made out of,

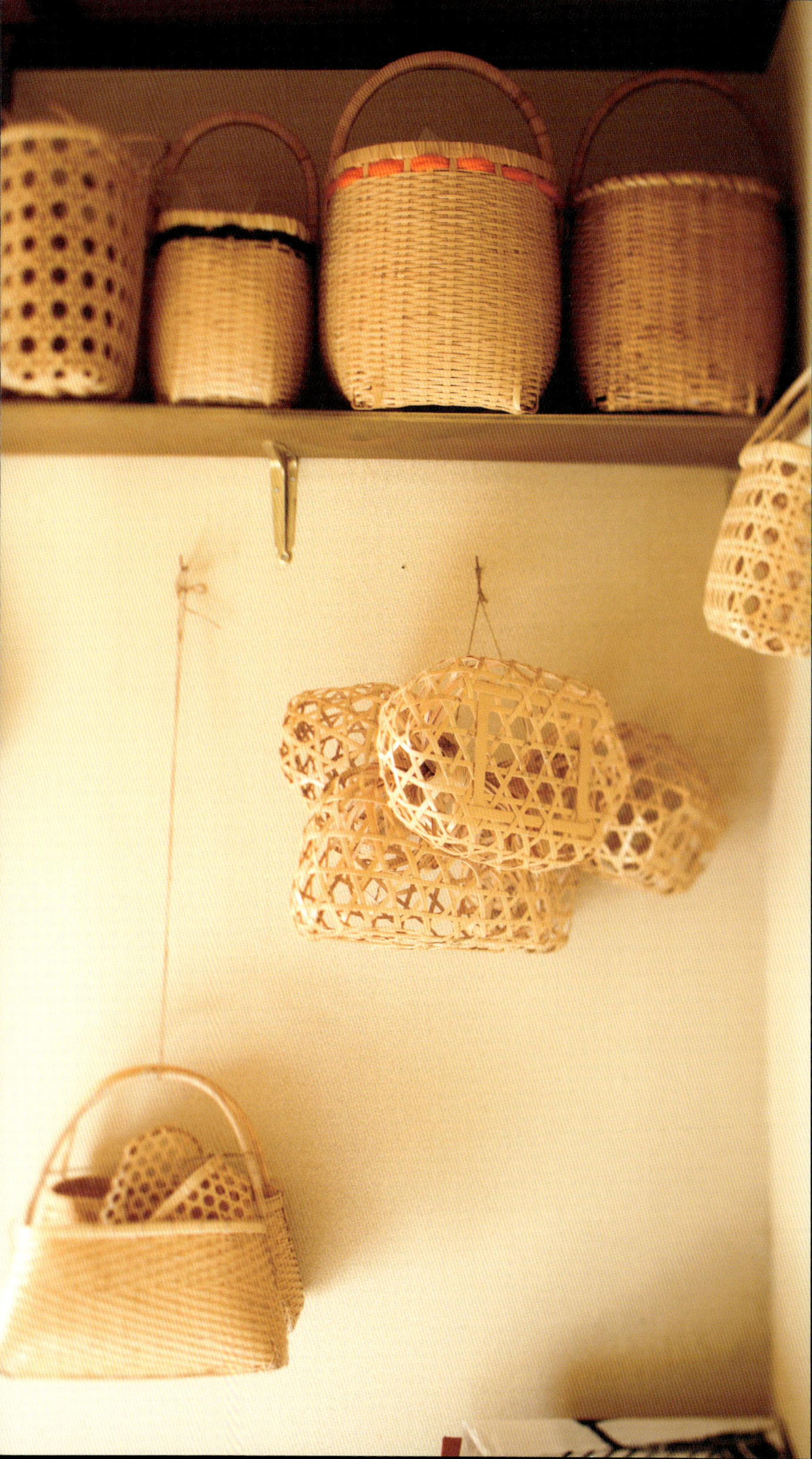

# 透かし網代編みのかごバッグ
Sukashi ajiro weave basket bag

柴田恵 作
By Megumi Shibata

細くしなやかなすず竹の良さを最大限に活かし、高い技術の手仕事で編まれる柴田恵さんの作品の中でも、かごバッグは人気アイテムのひとつです。
　「欲張りかもしれませんが、幅広い年齢、いろいろな服装、様々な用途と、あれにもこれにも違和感なく使い回しできるバッグを作りたいと思いました。透かし網代編みは、もとは水切り用のざるに使われていた編み方ですが、縁まで同じ編みにすることでおしゃれ感が出るのではと考えたのです」
　そして仕上がったのが、透かし網代編みのかごバッグ。今までにはないスタイリッシュさに、新しいかごの時代を予感した人は少なくありません。光にかざすと透かしの影が何とも美しい、柴田さんの作品ならではの上質な美を楽しめるかごバッグです。

Making the absolute best out of the fineness and sheen of the "suzutake" bamboo, this basket bag is one example of Megumi Shibata's highly-skilled handmade items.
"It may sound greedy, but I really wanted to make a basket that could be used by a range of ages, would go with a range of clothes, and could be used for a range of purposes without seeming out of place. Though the sukashi ajiro weave was originally used to drain zaru soba noodles, I thought that weaving the exact seem weave all the way to the edges would lend this basket a sense of stylishness."
And here's the finished sukashi ajiro basket bag. Not only is its stylishness on a level of that never seen before, there are plenty of people that feel that this basket is heralding in a new basket era. The shadow of the sukashi pattern looks beautiful as the light passes through it, and the basket as a whole possesses a fine beauty that is indicative of Shibata's work.

[ Chapter 1 ]

すず竹を四つ割りで保管しておくと、天候の関係でシミがついてしまう竹もある。これまでは使えないものとして処分していたが、材料としての強度などに何ら問題はない。そこで、「見た目の違和感をメリットに」という逆転の発想でデザインしたのが、写真の網代編みのかごバッグ（制作途中）。時間が経てばシミのひごは濃い飴色になるので、飴色の濃淡を楽しめる。

If suzutake is stored in quarters, some bamboo may develop splotching due to the weather. Until now this splotched bamboo was often dealt with as something unusable, but as a material there is no problem with its strength whatsoever. The basket that turned everything on its head with the idea of "using its strange appearance to its advantage" is the ajiro weave basket bag pictured (during production). If given enough time, the splotchy bamboo strips will take on a deep amber hue, so you can have fun with those shades.

# 桝網代バッグ
ます あじろ
Masu ajiro bag

中岩孝二 作
By Koji Nakaiwa

身体全体を道具のように使い、ひご作りをしている中岩さん。

Using the entirety of his mind and body as a tool, Nakaiwa makes a basket.

真竹を油抜きした晒し竹で作ったものを「白物」と言うのに対し、染色や漆塗りなどをほどこしたものは「黒物」と言われています。そして、竹工芸作家・中岩孝二さんの作品を、あえてジャンルで言うなら黒物です。

　34歳という若さで伝統工芸士を取得した技の持ち主である中岩さんが、自ら「技術の結集」と呼ぶのが、桝網代バッグ。細かい模様が美しい桝網代編みはとても難しい編み方ですが、網代編みを専門とし、その極みを目指す中岩さんにとっては一番好きな編み方だそうです。

　「素材には、染色では出にくい淡い色を求めて、炭化竹と呼ばれる炭化着色した真竹を選びました。表面は漆を何度も塗って仕上げたのですが、光沢のあるきれいな飴色は、とても気に入っています」

　内布は上質でつくられた巾着、紐は正紐を用いた、こだわりの逸品。炭化竹の作品は、数年経つとさらに艶が出てくるというから、使い続ける楽しみもふくらみます。

As products made from bleached madake bamboo with its oil extracted are called "shiromono", those which have been dyed or had lacquered applied to them are referred to as "kuromono". If Koji Nakaiwa's work had to be grouped into either of these categories, it would be "kuromono".

Gaining his Japanese traditional craftsman qualification at the tender age of 34, the skillful Nakaiwa himself refers to his masu ajiro bag as a "concentration of skill". Even though the finely-detailed and beautiful masu ajiro weave is a very difficult weave, it appears to be a firm favourite of Nakaiwa who as an expert in the ajiro weave and aims for the best.

"For the material, I wanted a faint colour that would be hard to achieve through dyeing, so I selected this "tankachiku" madake bamboo that's been dyed through carbonization. A lacquer is applied to the surface of the bamboo multiple times as a finish, but it still has a nice and glossy amber color that I really like."

The material inside is a fine-quality kinchaku pouch and good quality cord is used for a luxurious piece. Tankachiku goods tend to get a nice glaze after a few years, so you can expect a lot from long-term use.

# いろいろなかごバッグ
Various basket bags

## かごバッグ「空かご」
"Sora kago" basket bag

**児玉美重 作**
By Mie Kodama

四つ目の編み目に対角線になるように、交差したひごが通っている「差し四つ目編み」。それをベースに、斜めに片方だけ差す編み方にすることで、モダンな雰囲気を創っています。

A "sashi yotsume weave" that's made with yotsume stitches with diagonally incorporated strips. Using this as a base, a modern feel has been created by the diagonal strips that are inserted to slant in one direction.

## 亀甲崩し編みのかごバッグ
Kikko kuzuhi weave basket bag

**大谷健一 作**
By Kenichi Otani

亀甲編みは編み目がクレマチスの花に似ていることから、クレマチスの別名「鉄線」にちなんで「鉄線編み」とも呼ばれます。亀甲編みから1本ずつ抜いて編んだのが亀甲崩し編みです。

The stitches of the kikko weave resemble the clematis flower, meaning that it is sometimes also known as the "tessen weave", which is an alternative name for the clematis flower. When the kikko weave is woven by missing out one strip at a time, it becomes known as the kikko kuzushi weave.

## 根曲竹のかごバッグ
Nemagaridake basket bags

戸隠で見つけた、熟練職人の手仕事による逸品。燻製し飴色なった根曲竹のひごで作られています。

This was found in Togakushi and is a rare handcrafted beauty made by a very skillful craftsman. It's made from nemagaridake bamboo strips that have been smoked to achieve an amber hue.

## 山路編みのバッグ
### Yamaji weave bag

**清水貴之 作**
By Takayuki Shimizu

山の道を斜めに登るように見える「山路編み」。シンプルなラインが美しい小ぶりのバッグは、「浴衣に合わせたい」という20代から年配の方まで、幅広い世代に支持されています。

As the stitches look almost as if they're climbing the slopes of a mountain road, this weave is called the "yamaji weave". "Yamaji" means "mountain road" in Japanese. This smallish bag is enjoyed by people of all ages, from the 20-something who wants to pair it with their yukata, to the elderly.

## ふわり
### Fuwari

**清水貴之 作**
By Takayuki Shimizu

ふんわりした感じのかごバッグを作ってみたいと「差し六つ目編み」という編み方をアレンジして制作。差し六つ目は六つ目にひごを差し入れていく技法です。

This basket was made because of the desire to create a softer looking basket bag by adjusting the "sashi mutsume weave". The sashi mutsume weave is a technique achieved by threading strips of bamboo through a mutsume weave.

## 買いものかご
### Shopping basket

**撮影協力:縷縷(るる)**
Photos: Lulu

別府在住の竹工芸作家・森脇けい子さん作。底が広いので、卵やフルーツも横にして入れることができます。

By bamboo craftswoman Keiko Moriwaki, a resident of Beppu. Since the base of the basket is so wide, you can lie eggs and fruits in it flat.

# 花籠
## Hanakago

暮らしの道具だけでなく、観賞用の花入れなどにも竹かごは使われてきました。この場合、「花籠」と、かごを漢字で表記することが多いようです。

Not just a tool for everyday living, it's also used as a basket for showing off flowers among other uses. When used for flowers in Japan, the Japanese letters for basket in the title are often shown as a kanji character.

### 茶の湯と花籠 Hanakago and the tea ceremony

豊臣秀吉[※1]の小田原征伐が行われた1590年(天正18年)、この合戦にしたがった千利休(せんのりきゅう)[※2]が、竹に花を生けました。それが、竹筒花入れの始まりと伝わっています。以来、草の花入れとして竹筒が茶人に好まれるようになりました。千利休が提案した竹編みの花籠もまた、草の花入れとして茶人に好まれ、茶の湯の発展とともに室町時代末期から現在まで続いています。千利休は、京都の桂川で見つけた漁夫が使う道具の魚籠(びく)を、花入れに使えると直感。そのときに仕立てた花入れは、「桂籠花入(かつらかごはないれ)」とか「桂籠(かつらかご)」と呼ばれています。なにげないかごも、見立ての工夫で茶の道具になることを、利休が実証した逸話として語り継がれてきました。床などに直に置く「置き花入れ(おきはないれ)」の他に、柱や壁に掛ける「掛け花入れ(かけはないれ)」があります。効果的に使用したのは古田織部(ふるたおりべ)[※3]とも言われ、室町時代には掛け花入れが大流行しました。

※1　戦国時代から安土桃山時代にかけての武将。天下人。
※2　戦国時代から安土桃山時代にかけての茶人。千家流茶道の開祖。
※3　戦後時代から江戸時代初期にかけての武将。織部は茶人としての名。
　　　千利休亡き後、茶の湯の世界でリーダー的存在となる。

Sen no Rikyu(*1), who was present at Hideyoshi Toyotomi's(*2) Siege of Odawara in 1590, used to arrange flowers in bamboo. It's said that this is the beginning of bamboo pipe hanaire. Since then, bamboo pipes have become well loved by masters of the tea ceremony as plant hanaire. The bamboo woven hanakago that Sen no Rikyu suggested also became well liked as a plant hanaire by the masters of tea ceremony and has been in use ever since the late Muromachi era, from when the tea ceremony was developed. Sen no Rikyu had a hunch that the wicker biku fishing basket that he found a fisherman using in Katsuragawa, near Kyoto, could be used as a hanaire. The hanaire that were made at that time are called "katsurakago hanaire" or "katsurakago". The anecdote that even a plain basket could become a tool in the tea ceremony through good selection has been passed down as an anecdote proven by Sen no Rikyu. There are also hanaire that are put directly on the floor (oki hanaire), as well as those that hang on walls and posts (kake hanaire). It's said that the person that used them most effectively was called Oribe Furuta(*3) and kake hanaire were extremely popular during the Muromachi era.

*1 A master of tea ceremony who lived through the warring states and Azuchi-Momoyama periods. The founder of the Senke school of tea ceremony.
*2 A shogun who lived through the warring states and Azuchi-Momoyama periods. A ruler.
*3 A military commander who lived through the warring states period until the beginning of the Edo period. "Oribe" is his name as a master of tea ceremony. He became somewhat of a world leader of tea ceremony after Sen no Rikyu passed away.

# 花籠 宝珠
Hanakago hoju

**中岩孝二 作**
By Koji Nakaiwa

　竹工芸作家の中岩孝二さんが、大好きな椿の花を生けるために作ったのが「花籠宝珠」。もちろん、用途は椿の花に限定されるわけではありません。撮影時は椿の季節では無かったので野の花を生けたところ、その美しさが自然に引き出されました。波網代（なみあじろ）編みで編まれた胴部分に使われているのは、晒し竹を玉ねぎの皮で染色したひご。中岩さんが自ら考え染めたもので、つややかな美しい飴色をしています。そして、底の補強に使用したのは煤竹（すすだけ）。煤竹は、長い年月をかけて囲炉裏の煙でいぶされ、自然に茶褐色になった竹のことで、貴重でかつ高価でもあります。さらに、縁には煤竹の中でも貴重な鳳尾竹（ほうびちく）を使うなど、椿の花の魅力を最大限に生かすための工夫が、編み方、材料、形にいたるまで、細部になされています。

The bamboo craftsman Koji Nakaiwa created this "haanakago hoju" to arrange his beloved camellia flowers in. Of course, this basket isn't just limited to camellia flowers, and as it wasn't the season for camellia flowers when this shot was taken, wildflowers were used instead, bringing the beauty out naturally.Bleached bamboo strips that have been dyed with onion skin were used for the trunk of the basket, which is woven with a nami ajiro weave. Dyed based on Nakaiwa's own design, it has a glossy amber colour to it.In addition, the support in the base is made from susudake bamboo. Susudake bamboo naturally turns a reddish-brown over the years as it gets smoked by smoke from the hearth, and is both precious and expensive. Furthermore, by using hobichiku bamboo on the rim alongside the susudake, and by considering all the fine details from the weave, to the materials and shape, the attractiveness of the camellias has been designed to be maximized from a range of angles.

[ Chapter 1 ]

# 花籠 白雲

Hanakago shirakumo

## 児玉美重 作
By Mie Kodama

　工芸作品の制作にも意欲的な児玉さんは、晒し竹を磨いた新たな"白"にチャレンジし、「花籠 白雲」を完成させました。胴部分は、縄目編みの編み地に、縦にひごを刺す櫛目(くしめ)編みという編み方で、透けた状態を効果的に創り出しています。そして、風で揺らいでいる竹林の情景を、差しひごの削りのラインと回しひごのラインで表現。花入れとしてだけでなく、オブジェのように窓辺に置いたり、フロアライトにして、編み目の間からもれる光を楽しむこともできます。

Kodama, who is ambitious in her craft-making, was challenged to polish bleached bamboo to the point of getting a new "white" and came up with the "Hanakago shirakumo", meaning "white cloud". The trunk is comprised of the kushime weave, which is made by passing bamboo strips vertically through a nawame weave, effectively creating a gapped-stitch. A scene of a bamboo thicket swaying in the breeze is expressed through the torn line of the threaded-in bamboo strips and the strips that go around the basket. This basket isn't only used as a hanaire, but could also make a nice ornament for the windowsill or a beautiful floor light where the light pouring from the gaps in the stitching can be enjoyed.

# 一輪挿し
Ichirinzashi

**大谷健一 作**
By Kenichi Otani

　手軽さとかわいらしさから、人気がある一輪挿し。幅広い層に好まれているのが、やたら編みで編まれた大谷さんの一輪挿しです。「やたらめったら編み進む」ことから、その名がついたと言われる、やたら編みは、ダイナミックさもあって「乱れ編み」とも呼ばれます。編み方に決まりはない分、自分がどう編みたいのか、作り手の個性で独自の規則性が求められます。それだけに、作り手の独創性を楽しめる編み方でもあります。

Its simplicity and cuteness makes this one-flower ichirinzashi basket very popular. Liked on a number of levels, this is Otani's ichirinzashi that's woven with the yatara weave. The yatara weave, which is said to get its name from the Japanese word "yattaramettara", which means to do something carelessly and at random, has a certain dynamism and is also called the "midare weave". For all the lack of definiton in the weave, it still requires some individual regularity from the maker's personality and thoughts about how they would like to weave it. Because of this you can enjoy each creator's ingenuity.

# 掛け花入れ
Kake hanaire

**清水貴之 作**
By Takayuki Shimizu

　柱や壁に掛けて使う掛け花入れとして作られましたが、テーブルなどに置いて使うこともできます。四つ目編みから派生した、菱（ひし）四つ目編みで編まれています。菱四つ目編みは、洗練された雰囲気が好まれて、花籠に使われることがよくあります。ねじれた柄のデザインが印象的な、美しい花籠に仕上がっています。

This basket was made as a kake hanaire to hang on the wall or a post, but it can also be placed on surfaces such as a table. It's woven with the hishi yotsume weave, which is a derivative of the yotsume weave. The hishi yotsume weave is well-liked for its polished feel and is often used in the weaving of hanakago. The twisted design completes this beautiful and impressive basket.

# 茶籠など
## Chakago and others

## 千筋提籃二段重
### 2 -tiered sensuji teiran

**桑原健次郎 作**

By Kenjiro Kuwabara

提籃（ていらん）は煎茶道で使う茶道具一式を収納する籠。桑原哲次郎さんの父・健次郎さん（故人）の作品。染料には化学染料ではない昔の顔料が使われています。

A teiran is a basket used in sencha tea ceremony to store all of the tea utensils. This is an item made by the father of Tetsujiro Kuwabara, Kenjiro (deceased). Traditional pigments are used in the dyes instead of chemical colourings.

## 御所籠
### Gosho kago

**中岩孝二 作**

By Koji Nakaiwa

漆塗りで仕上げ、組紐は江戸組紐の老舗・偕可園のものを使用。御所籠は、茶道具一式を納めて持ち歩くための籠ですが、宝石箱など、他の用途で利用する人も少なくありません。

Finished with lacquer and braided cord from the old Edo-era cord shop, Kaikaen. Gosho kago are baskets that are used to store and carry full sets of tea utensils, but there are also plenty of people who use them as jewelry boxes and for other uses.

## 姫玉手箱
### Hime tamatebako

**中岩孝二 作**

By Koji Nakaiwa

胴と蓋には煤竹を使用（胴は網代編み、蓋は連続桝網代編み）。箱の内側は玉ねぎ染めのひごを使って波網代編みで仕上げています。大切な物を保管する箱として使われています。

The trunk and lid are both made with susudake (the trunk woven with an ajiro weave, and the lid woven with a renzoku masu ajiro weave.) The interior is finished with onion-stained bamboo strips woven into a nami ajiro weave. This basket is often used as a box in which to keep precious objects.

Chapter 1

061

# ファッションアイテム

Fashion accessories

## ピアス「ツイスト」

"Twist" piercing

### 清水貴之 作

By Takayuki Shimizu

弾力を活かし、竹ひごをねじったり丸めたりして作ったピアス。上の大ぶりなものは、涙や雫をイメージしています。

This is a piercing that has been twisted and rolled to make the most of the flexibility of the bamboo strips. The large object on top is was made with the image of a tear drop and droplets in mind.

## ペンダント

Pendant

### 清水貴之 作

By Takayuki Shimizu

清水さんは、竹ひごで作った箸置きを見たお客様から「紐をつけてペンダントにしたりストラップにするとかわいいかも」と言われたのをヒントに、アクセサリーを作り始めたそうです。

Shimizu got the idea to start making accessories from a customer who commented that the chopstick stand that he had made out of bamboo strips would "look cute if made into a pendant or put on a strap".

## 竹チョーカー、竹ブレス

Bamboo choker & bamboo bracelet

### 児玉美重 作

By Mie Kodama

「目の詰まったデザインにしたかったので、六つ目ベースの網代編みで仕上げました」と児玉さん。縁は革で加工し、リボンをあしらうなど、異素材との組み合わせがよりおしゃれ感を創っています。

"I wanted to give them an eye-catching design so I gave them a mutsume weave base, with an ajiro weave finish," says Kodama. The edges are finished with leather, or arranged with a ribbon, giving this combination of bamboo and another material a more stylish feel.

[ Chapter 1 ]

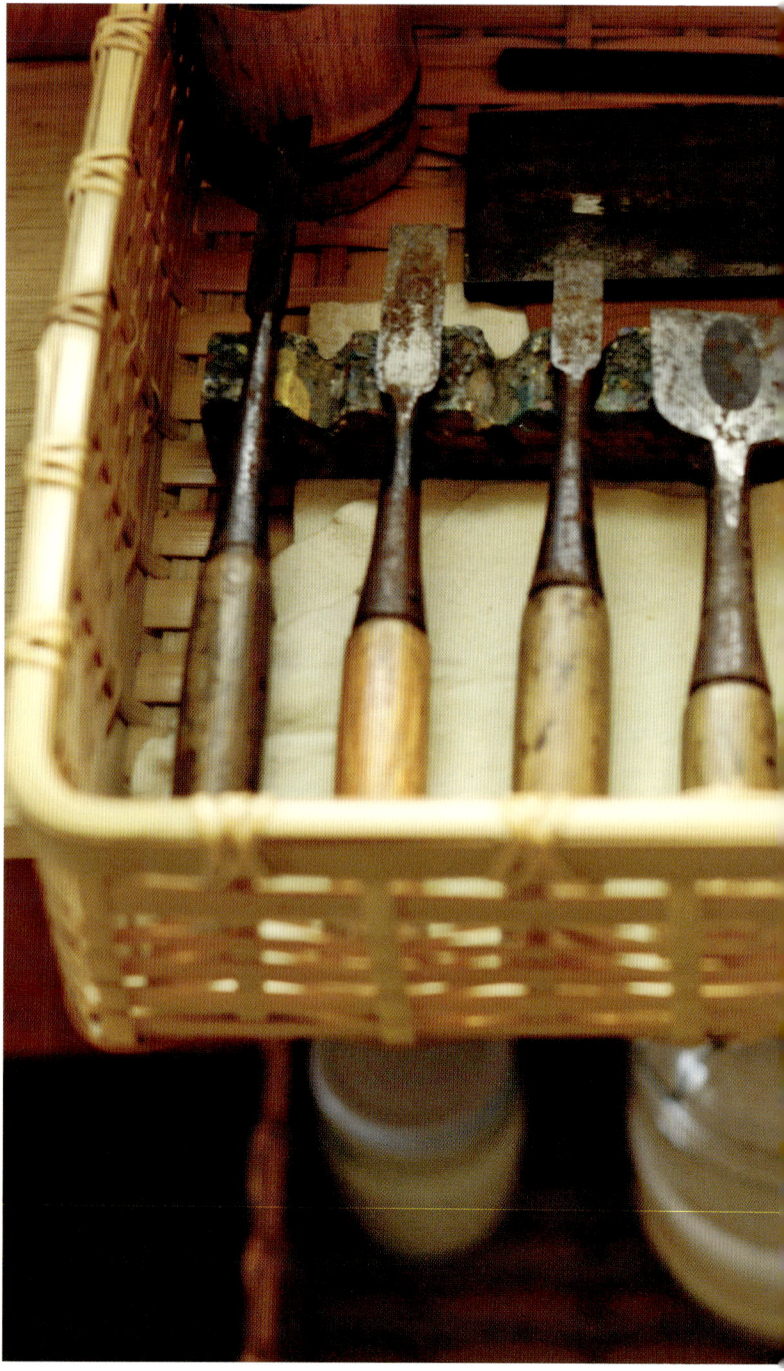

Chapter 1

## Chapter 2

# 竹かごの基礎知識
#### Bamboo basket basic knowledge

日本には、およそ600種類の竹が
自生していると言われています。
そのうち竹かごの材料になるのは約30種類。
「日本の竹」の特徴の他、
日本の文化やライフスタイルの変化の中で、
竹かごがどのように使われてきたのかを紹介します。

It's said that as many as 600 types of bamboo
grow in Japan. Within that number,
roughly 30 types can be used to make bamboo baskets.
As well as the characteristics of "Japanese bamboo",
we'll be introducing how the use of
bamboo baskets has changed as Japanese culture
and lifestyles continue to evolve.

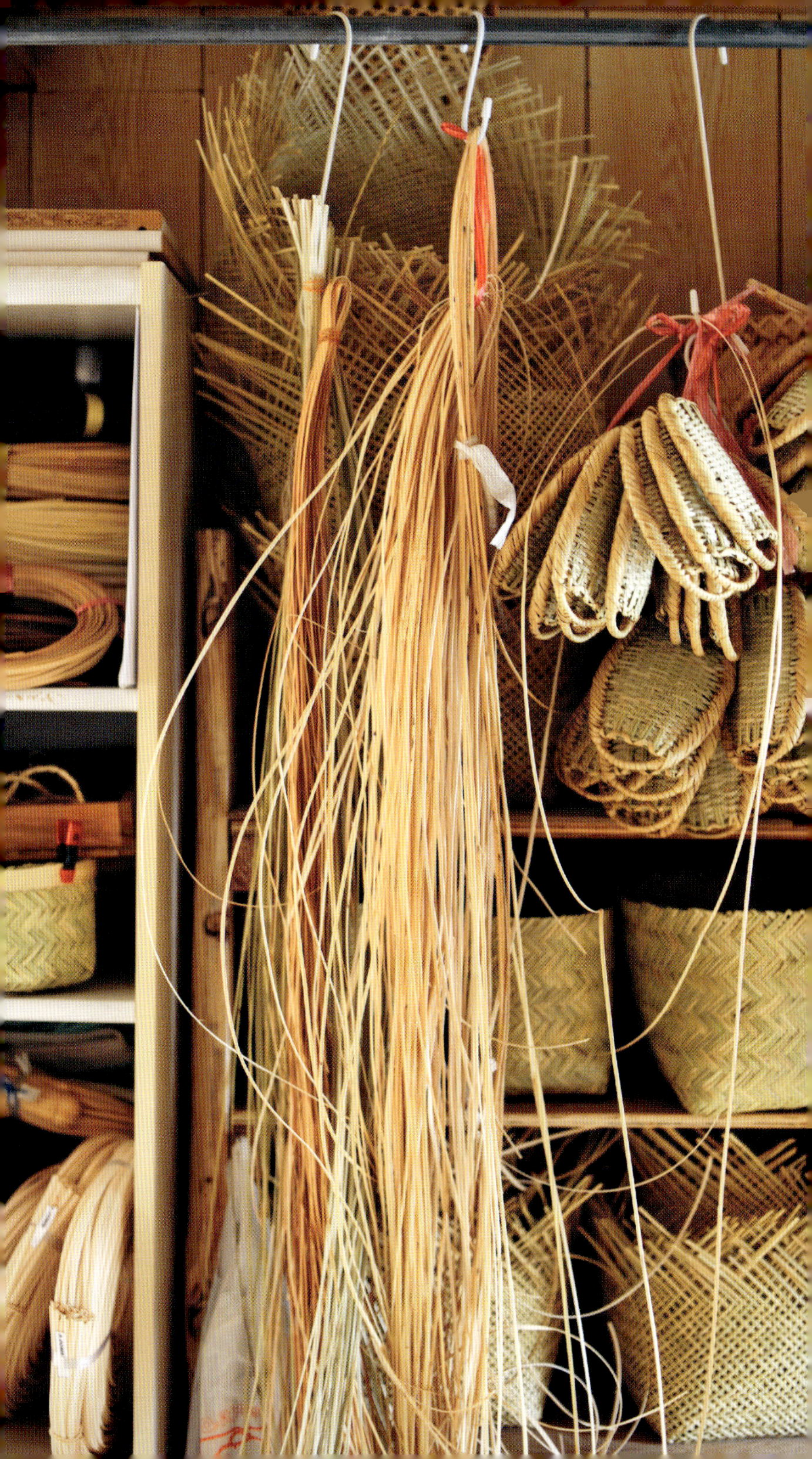

# 日本の竹
Japanese bamboo

## 竹の種類
Types of Bamboo

　世界には約1,200種類の竹があり、東南アジア、オーストラリア、中南米、アフリカなどの温暖な地域に広く分布しています。日本ではそのうち約600種類が自生していると考えられており、中でもよく見るのは、真竹（マダケ）・孟宗竹（モウソウチク）・淡竹（ハチク）。内訳は真竹6割・孟宗竹2割・淡竹1割で、全体の9割を占めています。この3種類は「三大有用竹」とも呼ばれ、暮らしの道具のみならず建材などにも幅広く利用されてきました。

In the world there are approximately 1,200 types of bamboo, distributed over areas with warm climates, such as those in South East Asia, Australia, and Africa. It's thought that around 600 of those species grow in Japan, and within those the most commonly seen types are madake, mosochiku, and hachiku bamboo. Madake makes up 60% of used bamboo, with 20% mosochiku, and 10% hachiku, meaning these 3 types total 90% of all Japanese bamboo use. These three types of bamboo are also known as the "3 Most Useful Bamboo" and are not only made into tools for daily living, but are also utilized in architecture and have a wide range of other uses.

## 竹と笹
Bamboo & Bamboo grass

　竹と笹は、植物学的には竹の皮のはがれ方に違いがあり、生長するとタケノコの皮がはがれるものが竹、生長しても皮がはがれないものが笹です。日本には、矢竹（ヤダケ）のように名前は竹でも笹類に分類されるものがあれば、阿亀笹（オカメザサ）のように名前は笹でも竹類に分類されるものがあります。

Bamboo and bamboo grass are differentiated in botany by the way that their bark peels off. If you can peel the bark off the shoots when it grows then it's bamboo, whereas if you cannot peel off the bark even if it grows, it's bamboo grass. In Japan, even though some bamboo species may have names such as yadake that include the Japanese word for bamboo ("take"), they're actually bamboo grass, and vice versa, some types of bamboo such as okamezasa may have the Japanese word for bamboo grass ("sasa") in the title, but are actually species of bamboo.

熊本県の孟宗竹の竹林。
A mosochiku bamboo thicket in Kumamoto Prefecture.

## 竹類・笹類の分類　Classification of Bamboo & Bamboo grass

**【竹類】Bamboo**
真竹（マダケ）
Madake
孟宗竹（モウソウチク）
Mosochiku
淡竹（ハチク）
Hachiku
黒竹（クロチク）
Kurochiku

雲紋竹（ウンモンチク）
Unmonchiku
土佐虎斑竹（トサトラフダケ）
Tosatorafudake
阿亀笹（オカメザサ）
Okamezasa
東根笹（アズマネザサ）
Azumanezasa

**【笹類】Bamboo grass**
千島笹（チシマザサ）
※別名:根曲竹（ネマガリダケ）
Chishimazasa (also known as "nemagaridake")
熊笹（クマザサ）
Kumazasa
矢竹（ヤダケ）
Yadake

# 日本の竹の特性
Characteristics of Japanese Bamboo

## 良質な材料だった竹
Bamboo that made good-quality material

　竹は茎が空洞になっており、この茎のことを稈と言います。空洞である分、軽量ですが、それにも関わらず強さがあり、弾力性に富みしなやかで、割裂性に優れているのが竹の特性です。竹には抗菌作用があるとされてきたことも、日用品や工芸品に竹が利用された背景にありました。身近にあるという理由だけではなく良材であった竹は、生活に欠かせない材料として日本人に親しまれてきました。

The stem of the bamboo is hollow, and is called a "culm". Though this hollow inside makes the stem light-weight, it has no impact on its great strength, elasticity, suppleness, and clevability, which are all qualities of Japanese bamboo. The thought that bamboo has an antibacterial effect has also led to its use in handicrafts and everyday items. Bamboo has been adopted so enthusiastically by Japanese people not only due to its proximity, but also because good-quality bamboo was a material that was essential for their everyday lives.

## 昔話でも語られた竹の生長の早さ
The Legendary Speed of Bamboo Growth

　竹は木と同様に身近にある材料として、古くから利用されてきました。日本人なら誰もが知っている昔話のひとつに『竹取物語』がありますが、物語の中で竹から生まれたかぐや姫は3カ月であっという間に大人になりました。現実に竹の生長はとても早く、春に芽を出しタケノコとして育つと1日に数十㎝も伸び、夏には成竹になり生涯の背丈や太さが決まります。

Bamboo has been used since the distant past much like wood, another close-at-hand material. All Japanese people know "The Tale of the Bamboo Cutter", and how Princess Kaguya was born from inside some bamboo before growing into an adult in just 3 months. In reality, the growth rate of bamboo is very fast as well. Sprouting in spring, once these plants reach the bamboo shoots stage they often grow a number of centimetres per day, before finally becoming full-grown bamboo in the summer, where they will reach their final height and thickness.

空洞になっている。
The inside is hollow.

# 竹かごに使われる竹
Bamboo used in bamboo baskets

最も使われるのは、竹かご作りに適した性質を持ち、数も多い真竹です。けれど寒い土地では真竹は育ちにくいため、東北地方などでは身近にあった根曲竹やすず竹などが使われてきました。

The most used type of bamboo is madake which is the most plentiful and the best suited to bamboo basket making. However, madake is hard to grow in colder climates, so bamboo species such as Nemagaridake or Suzutake have come to be used in colder areas like North-East Japan.

---

### 真竹 Madake

高さは約10m、直径10cm前後になる大型の竹です。粘り気があり曲げやすく、割りそぎもしやすいという優れた特性を持つ真竹は、竹かご作りに最もよく使われます。節が低くて節間が長く、表面に光沢があり、弾力性に富んだ竹が良質とされています。一般的に伐採時期は、竹の水揚げが止まる秋から冬までの期間が適していると言われています。

At approximately 10m tall and 10cm in diameter, madake is a very large-sized type of bamboo. Its exceptional qualities, such as being tacky, pliable, and easy to cut and tear, mean that it's the most used bamboo for bamboo basket making. With its short nodes and long internodes, shiny surface, and flexibility it's considered to be good quality. It's said that the time to cut down madake bamboo should generally be between fall, when the bamboo harvest ends, and winter.

---

### 孟宗竹 Mosochiku

日本で生育している竹の中では最大で、高さ20m以上、直径20cmになるものもあります。見た目は真竹に似ていますが、真竹の節が二重の輪になる（二環状）なのに対し、孟宗竹の節は一重の輪（単環状）です。建築材や垣根などに使われますが、肉厚でしなりがある特性を活かし、お箸やカトラリーにも使われます。

Out of the types of bamboo that grow in Japan, there is one that grows up to 20m in height and 20cm in diameter. Though it resembles madake, madake nodes have 2 rings (double-ringed) whereas mosochiku have 1 (single-ringed). Though often used in architecture and fences, the strong yet pliable properties of this bamboo are utilized to make chopsticks and cutlery too.

## 黒竹  Kurochiku

和歌山県や高知県で見られます。高さ4m前後、直径2〜3cmの中型の竹です。稈の美しさから竹細工に使われる他、観賞用として坪庭などの植栽に好まれます。

Found in Wakayama and Kochi Prefectures. At around 4 m tall and 2-3 cm in diameter, this is a medium sized species of bamboo. As the culm is so beautiful it's not only used in bamboo work and is much loved as a plant to raise and admire in the garden.

## 矢竹  Yadake

本州から九州まで各地で生息します。高さは3〜4m、直径1cmほどです。筆軸や扇子などに使われてきました。

This grows all over from the Japanese islands of Honshu to Kyushu. It has a height of 3-4 m and a diameter of 1 cm. It's often used in writing brushes and folding fans.

## 虎斑竹  Torafudake

高知県の一定地域に生育するので土佐虎斑竹とも呼ばれます。黒竹の変種で茶色の斑紋が特徴です。

As it only grows in a specific area of Kochi Prefecture, it's also known as Tosatorafudake. A mutation of kurochiku, it's distinguished by its brown speckles.

## 阿亀笹  Okamezasa

関東以西の各地に分布。高さは1〜2mと小型の竹です。稈はしなりやすく強靭なので、小さなかごや器を編むことができます。

Found all over areas to the west of the Kanto region, this is a small species of bamboo that grows to 1-2 m tall. The culm is pliable and tough, making it possible to weave into small baskets and containers.

## すず竹  Suzutake

背丈が2m程度、直径5〜8mmの細い竹。寒い地域で育ちやすく、しなやかで、折り曲げても元に戻りやすいのが特徴です。

A slender species of bamboo with a height of 2 m and a diameter of just 5-8 mm. It's easy to grow in colder regions and is flexible enough to return to its original shape when bent.

[ Chapter 2 ]

### 篠竹 Shinodake

背丈は3m程度で、直径2cm程度の細い竹です。山地に群生し、柔軟で弾力があるのが特徴です。日本有数の篠竹細工の産地である岩出山（宮城県大崎市）では、市内でも自生しています。

Another slender bamboo at 3m tall and 2cm wide. It's known for growing en masse in mountainous regions and for its flexibility and elasticity. It grows wild inside the town of Iwadeyama (Osaki, Miyagi Prefecture), which is famous for producing Japan's most prominent Shinodake crafts.

### 根曲竹 Nemagaridake

学名はチシマザサ。根に近いところが曲がっているところから、根曲竹と呼ばれるようになりました。高さ4mになることもあります。

Its scientific name is chishimazasa. As the parts of the bamboo near the roots curve it has also become known as "nemagaridake" (which roughly translates into "twisted root bamboo" in English). Nemagaridake can reach heights of up to 4 m.

## 【加工された竹】 Processed bamboo

### 晒し竹 Bleached bamboo

竹に含まれる油を抜き天日で干した竹のことで、白竹（しらたけ）とも呼ばれます。材料には、良質な真竹が選ばれます。

This is bamboo that has had the oil removed from it and has been dried in the sun, and is also called "shiratake". Good-quality madake bamboo is chosen to make it.

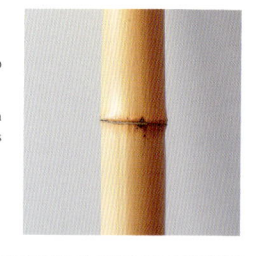

### 煤竹 Susudake

長年、囲炉裏の煤でいぶされて色が変色した竹のことを言います。希少価値が高いため大変高価です。煤竹は、茶道具や花籠、高級なかごバッグなどに使われます。

This is bamboo that has changed colour after being smoked by a hearth for a number of years. As this bamboo is so scarce, it is also very expensive. Susudake is used for tea ceremony utensils, hanakago, and luxury basket bags.

### 炭化竹 Tankachiku

煤竹が手に入りにくいため、人工的に作る炭化竹が代用されるようになりました。高温高圧で炭化させて作ります。煤竹ほどではないにしても、加工に費用がかかるため炭化竹も高価です。

As susudake is so hard to get hold of, manmade carbonized bamboo (tankachiku) is often substituted. It's made by carbonizing the bamboo at high pressures and temperatures. Though it is not as expensive as susudake, it still costs a lot to produce, which is reflected in the price tag.

---

※撮影協力「別府市竹細工伝統産業会館」
*Photos from "Beppu Traditional Bamboo Craft & Industry Hall"

# 竹かごの各部の名称

Naming each section of a bamboo basket

### 縁 Rim

縁まわり。使うときに手がよく触れる部分なので、耐久性や手触りに配慮した縁作りが求められる。また、目を引くところでもあるので、作家の作品にはワンポイントになるようなデザインの工夫が見られる。

This is the rim that runs along the edge. As this is often touched by hands when in use, it needs to be somewhat durable and care needs to be paid to the feel. In addition, this area can also be used to attract the eye, so you can see accents in the design placed there by wily makers.

### 胴 Trunk

側面のところを胴と言う。「四つ目編みかご」とか「六つ目編みのかごバッグ」など、かごの名前に編みの名前がついているものがよくあるが、その場合は、胴の編み方をさしている。

The outside area of the basket is called the trunk. There are many types of basket, such as the "yotsume weave basket" and "mutsume weave basket bag", that contain the name of the weaves that they use in their titles. The name always refers to the weave of the trunk.

### 腰 Koshi

底から胴へ立ちあげるところを「腰」と呼ぶ。

The area that transitions from the base to the trunk is called the "koshi".

### 底 Base

かごの底部分。一般的に竹かごは底から編んでいくが、底編みと胴編みが違うかごもある。

This is the bottom of the basket. Baskets are usually woven from the base upwards, but there are some baskets that have different weaves for the trunk and base.

### 力竹（ちからだけ）Bamboo supports

底を補強するときに使う。

Used to strengthen the base.

---

## かご編みの工程　The basket weaving process

**❶底編み** Weaving the base
底になる部分を編む。

The part that will form the base of the basket is woven.

**❷立ち上げる** Building upwards
立ち上げる工程のことを「腰立ち」と言う。きれいな形を構成するのに技術を要する重要な工程。

The process of standing up the bamboo is called "koshidachi". This is an important step that requires technique to construct a nice-looking shape.

**❸胴編み** Weaving the trunk
作り手の表現力が強調されるところでもあり、複数の編み方を組み合わせて作品を仕上げることも少なくない。

This where the maker can exert their expressiveness, and there are lots of examples of people even combining 2 kinds of weave to make an item here.

**❹縁** Rim
最後に「縁」を仕上げて完成。

Lastly, a rim is added and the basket is complete.

# 竹かごの歴史
History of bamboo baskets

## 数千年前から、竹かごは作られていた
Bamboo baskets have been made from thousands of years ago

　日本の暮らしと竹との関係はとても古く、縄文時代のものと思われる竹かごが発掘されていることから、その歴史は数千年前にまでさかのぼると考えられています。また、奈良時代を中心とした美術工芸品を収蔵している正倉院でも、竹工芸品が発見されました。こうした背景からも、日本では、竹工芸の高度な技術が育まれてきたことが分かります。また安土桃山時代には、千利休によって、竹かごが花を生ける器として使われるようになります。さらに江戸時代中頃になると、花を生ける花籠が広まり、格調の高い中国風の作品などが盛んに作られました。

The relationship between Japanese living and bamboo baskets is long, and from excavated bamboo baskets that are thought to be from the Jomon period, it's thought that this history stretches back for thousands of years. These baskets can also be found in the Shosoin, which contains arts and crafts mainly from the Nara period. From this background, you can see that Japan has been able to rear high bamboo craft skills.Furthermore, these bamboo baskets also began to be used as vessels for flower arrangement thanks to "Sen no Rikyu" in the Azuchi-Momoyama period. Then, in the middle of the Edo period, hanakago, which were used to arrange flowers, began to spread, and lots of Chinese-style, highly-dignified looking baskets were produced.

## 暮らしの道具に見出された"用の美"
The "beauty of use" found in everyday items for living

　一方では、農漁業や日用品などに使われる「暮らしの道具」が、日本の各地で作られていました。その技は明治に入ってからも、名もない職人たちによって継がれていました。そうした手仕事に、明治末から大正期に柳宗悦（やなぎむねよし）［※1］らが唱えた民藝運動によって光が照らされ、用の美が見出されます。

　昭和に入ると戦争中の物資不足もあり、竹を利用した製品が多種多様に作られるようになりました。そして戦後は経済成長を背景にたくさんのかごが作られたのですが、1960年代頃から大量生産のプラスチック製品におされ、竹かごの需要が激減してしまいます。

"Tools for everyday living", such as those that were made for agriculture and as household items, were made in every region throughout Japan. Even during the Meiji period, these skills were passed down by unnamed craftsmen. This hand-made work finally came to the forefront during the late Meiji period and early Taisho period thanks to Muneyoshi Yanagi's(*1) folk art movement, where its "beauty in use" was noticed.

As the country progressed into the Showa period it was at war, there was a massive shortage of materials and this is where the use for bamboo baskets started to diversify. Plenty of baskets were still being produced after the war in the period of rapid economic growth, but by the 60's the demand for mass-produced plastic products had eclipsed that of bamboo baskets, and demand for baskets fell steeply.

※1 民藝運動を起こした思想家、美学者、宗教哲学者。
*1 A thinker, aesthetician, and philosopher who started the folk art movement.

## デザイン性に富んだ別府竹工芸が登場
The appearance of well-designed Beppu bamboo crafts

　そうした苦難の時期に大分県の別府でおこったのが、「別府クラフト」です。そもそも別府竹細工の歴史は古く、江戸時代、湯治客が使った厨房用品の「ざる」や「かご」をお土産として持ち帰ったことから、「別府の竹かご」が広く知られるようになりました。明治以降は漆塗りの技術を用いた茶道具や花籠も作られ、昭和になると生野祥雲斎が人間国宝となり竹工芸を芸術の域まで高めました。

　こうした歴史的背景も後押しとなり、別府クラフトを機に、新しいライフスタイルを意識したデザイン性に富んだかごや器が作られるようになります。その流れは現在にも受け継がれ、別府ゆかりの若手作家のオリジナリティあふれる制作活動につながっています。

These "Beppu crafts", from the city of Beppu in Oita Prefecture, could make it seem like this period of hardship never even happened. The history of Beppu bamboo crafts has always been long, but after patrons to the hot springs took home kitchenware such as zaru plates and baskets as souvenirs, Beppu bamboo work became known far and wide. Since the Meiji period, the region has produced tea utensils and hanakago with lacquer techniques, and one if its craftsmen, Ikuno Shounsai, became a living national treasure, raising bamboo's status as an art form.

Supported by this historical background, and starting the Beppu crafts, many highly-designed baskets and containers were produced that were aware of the modern lifestyle. This flow of events continues to this day and into the highly-original creations of the young craftsmen of the young craftsmen of Beppu.

# Chapter 3

# 竹材を用意する

Preparing the bamboo

良いかごを作るには
良い竹ひごを作ることが不可欠です。
そして当然のことながら、良い竹ひごを作るには、
良い竹を選ぶことが重要な条件です。
ここでは、真竹を例に、竹を伐採するところから
晒し竹を作る工程を紹介します。
「Ⅰ 竹を伐る」では自ら竹を伐って
青物を制作している勢司恵美さんの仕事ぶりを、
「Ⅱ 晒し竹を作る」では、
別府で90年以上の歴史を持つ
永井製竹を見学させていただきました。

To make a quality bamboo basket,
it's essential to make quality bamboo strips.
Naturally therefore, to make good quality bamboo strips
you must select good quality bamboo.
Here we will introduce all of the steps from felling
the bamboo to making bleached bamboo,
using madake bamboo as an example.
For "Step 1: Felling the bamboo",
we learned from Emi Seishi,
who cuts her own bamboo to create aomono,
and for "Step 2: Making bleached bamboo",
we learned from over 90 years of expertise found at
Beppu-based Nagai Seichiku Bamboo store.

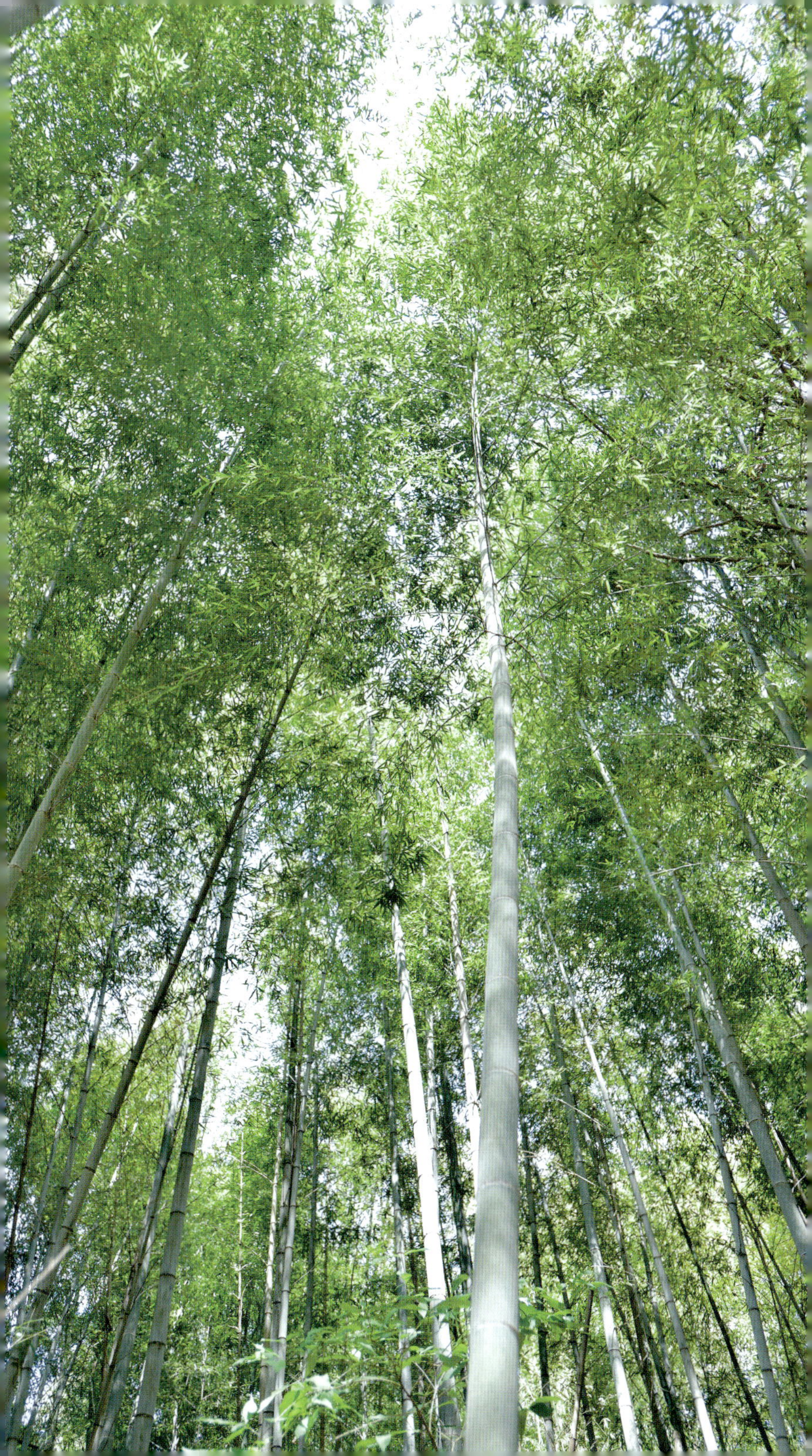

# I 竹を伐る
Felling the bamboo

## 伐採時期
The felling period

　竹の活動期は水分・養分が多く、この時期に伐った竹を用いると、かごになってから虫がついたりします。真竹の伐採はタケノコが出る時期が最も悪いとされ、伐り始めていいのは8月のお盆すぎ。ただし、そのまま置いておくとすぐに腐っていくので、早めに割り剥ぎをして、「竹ひご」にしてしまわなければなりません。

　地域によって差はありますが、休息期の10〜12月にまとめて伐り、以降はストックしてある竹を使います。とはいえ春を過ぎ暖かくなると、置き竹も腐っていきます。青物は、自然の摂理にそった竹との付き合いです。

During the active period of the bamboo it contains lots of moisture and nutrients, and if cut down during this time, will attract bugs even after it has been made into a basket. It's said that the worst time to cut down madake is when the bamboo shoots are out, and the earliest time to start is late-August. However, left in its present state, madake will start to rot quickly, so after it has been cut down it must be cut, torn, and made into bamboo strips as soon as possible.

Though it differs by region, the madake is felled all at once during the inactive period (October-December) and is stored for later. However if spring passes and it starts to get warmer, this stored bamboo will start to rot. Being made of bamboo, "aomono" is still at the mercy of nature's cycles.

## 竹の年齢
Age of the bamboo

　竹は6月頃に芽を出してタケノコとして育つと、1日に何十cmも伸びるほどの早さで生長します。1年目の竹は「1年生」「新竹（しんたけ）」「新子（しんこ）」と呼ばれ、肉質がやわらかくしなやかなので縁巻に利用されます。竹かご作りに適しているのは、3、4年目の竹だと言われています。

When bamboo is 6 months old it grows into a bamboo shoot, where it will quickly gain several centimeters of height per day. Bamboo in its first year of life is referred to as either "shintake" or "shinko", and as the flesh of the bamboo is so supple and glossy, it's often used for wrapping around the rim of the baskets. It's said that the bamboo most suited to baskets is in its 3rd or 4th year.

## 竹林を選ぶ
Selecting the bamboo grove

　「日があまりあたらない北斜面で育った竹がいい」「杉木立の間に立つ竹は、杉に負けないように育とうとするため伸びがよく、まっすぐで良い姿をしている」という話を耳にします。例えば勢司さんは「番傘を持って歩けるくらいに、竹と竹の間にゆとりがある場所のものがいい」と聞いたこともあるそうです。

We heard that "bamboo that hasn't had much sunlight and has grown facing northwards is good" and that "bamboo that grows in Japanese cedar groves is also good as it has a good length and grows in a nice and straight form in order to compete with the trees". Seishi also told us that if there was enough space to walk comfortably through 2 bamboo with a bangasa umbrella open, that is also a good sign.

## 竹を選ぶ
Selecting the bamboo

　竹かご作りに適した竹とそうでないものがありますし、どのような作品を作るかによっても選ぶ竹は違ってきます。

There is bamboo that is suited to making bamboo trips and there is bamboo that isn't. The bamboo to select may also differ depending on what kind of object you would like to make.

竹ひご作りには、枝が生えていなかったところを使う。

When making bamboo strips, areas where branches haven't grown are used.

（左）節がぼこっと高くなっている。また、節下が茶色い。このような竹は使えない。
（右）左の写真に比べると、節は低い。けれど、節下は茶色くなってきているので、こうした竹もあまり使わない。

(Left) The nodes stick out too much and the area underneath is brown, so this bamboo cannot be used.
(Right) Compared to the photograph on the left, the nodes stick out less. However, the area underneath the nodes has become brown, so that bamboo cannot really be used either.

○印の竹は１年目。他の竹に比べて青々している。

The bamboo marked with a circle is in its first year of life. Compared to those around it, it's much greener.

○印の竹は３、４年目で、竹かご作りの適齢期の竹。

The bamboo marked with a circle is in its 3rd or 4th year, so it's the perfect age for making bamboo strips.

## 竹選びのチェックポイント

Bamboo selection checkpoints

**【1年目】**…青々している。タケノコの皮がついていたりする。
**【2年目】**…青さはまだ残っているが、表面に汚れが少しついている。
**【3、4年目】**…竹の表面がうっすら白っぽくなっている（洗えばきれいな青竹になる）。

新竹はゆするとビュンビュンとしなやかに動きますし、見た目も色鮮やかなので見分けはつきやすいです。より正確に把握したいときは、枝を見ます。竹類は葉が更新する際、古い葉は小枝を付けたまま落葉します。枝の先端部にある落葉した跡を数えれば、竹の年齢を推測することができます。

**【節間】**…節と節の間の長さのこと。上の方の節間が長いものが良いと言われています。
**【節】**…節がぼこっと高くなっていると材料作りのときに扱いにくいし、かごになったときボコボコしてしまいます。そうした竹は避け、節が低い竹を選びます。例えば竹林の外側にあるような竹は風にあたりやすいので、節が高くなっています。また、節の下が茶色くなっているのは古いので、そうした竹も選びません。
**【太さ】**…地面から130cmくらいのところが直径6cm前後くらいの竹を選ぶことが多いですが、作りたい「ひご」に合わせて竹の太さを選びます。

1 year...... Very green. There is still bark left from its bamboo shoot stage.
2 years..... Still quite green, but there are now a few stains on the surface.
3 and 4 years....... The surface of the bamboo has become faintly white (but will become a beautiful green if washed.)

If shintake is shaken, it moves with a certain elasticity and the colour is very bright, so it's very easy to tell apart. If you want a more precise understanding, check the branches. When bamboo species re-grow their leaves, the old leaves drop to the floor while still on their tiny twigs. If you count the remnants left behind by these falling twigs at the ends of the branches, you can guess the age of the bamboo.

Inter-nodal space...... This is the length between each of the nodes. Bamboo with longer space between the nodes at the top is said to be good.
Nodes...... If the nodes of the bamboo stick out too much, they will be hard to work with when making material, and be full of holes when processed into a basket. That kind of bamboo should be avoided, and one with nodes that don't stick up as much chosen. For example, bamboo that grows on the outskirts of thickets tends to get hit by the wind, so the nodes tend to stick up more. As well as this, bamboo that has brown areas under the nodes is old and should not be chosen.
Thickness...... Though bamboo that is around 6cm in diameter at 130cm up from the ground is selected quite often, you should choose the thickness based on the desired thickness of your bamboo strips.

# 伐採の手順
The felling process

**【道具】**ノコギリ／手袋
Tools: Saw / Gloves

1. 竹の上の方を見て、傾きをチェック。例えば左に少し倒れている場合、左側から切ると竹の重さでノコギリが押されて動かしにくいので、この場合は右側から切る。

   Look at the top of the bamboo and check for a lean. For example, if the bamboo is leaning slightly to the left, sawing from the left would be difficult as the weight of the tree would make it hard to push the saw in. In this case, it should be sawn from the right.

2. ノコギリで竹の下の方を伐る。

   Use a saw to cut the tree near the bottom.

3. 竹はやわらかいので、力いっぱいノコギリを引かなくてもあっという間に伐れた。

   Bamboo is soft, so even if you don't saw at full power, the tree will be down in no time.

4. 切り口に近い下の方を動かして倒す。

   Move the bamboo near the bottom where you sawed to push it over.

5. 上の方で竹の葉同士がからまるので、ゆっくりと倒していく。

   There may be twigs and leaves tangled together near the top, so push it over slowly.

6. 枝の方が使わないので切り落とす。

   The branches won't be used, so cut them off.

# II 晒し竹を作る
## Making bleached bamboo

撮影協力:永井製竹
photos from Nagai Seichiku Bamboo store

## 晒し加工をする理由
The reason for the bleaching process

　伐採した竹は時間の経過とともに色あせていきますし、直射日光があたるとさらに早く褐色してしまいます。晒し加工をすると青からクリーム色へと変化しますが、表面をいつまでも美しく保つことができます。晒し加工は一般に「油抜き」と言われていますが、油抜きされた竹は「晒し竹」「白竹」と呼ばれ、晒し竹で作るかごは「白物」と言います。

As felled bamboo loses its colour over time, if it's hit by sunlight, it will go brown even quicker. If the bamboo is bleached, it will transform from a green to a cream colour, but it is then possible to keep the surface looking good. The bleaching process is usually called "oil extraction", and bamboo that has gone through this process is referred to as "sarashi dake" or "shiratake". Baskets that use materials that have gone through this process are called "shiromono".

## 油抜きの方法
Oil extraction method

　大きくは「乾式油抜き」と「湿式油抜き」の2種類あります。竹材店で行われるのは湿式です。

**【乾式油抜き】**
　「火晒し」とも呼ばれる方法で、竹を火であぶって油分を出します。個人で油抜きを行う場合は、この方法でガスコンロなどを利用したりします。網をのせてから稈をかざして熱すると、透明な油が浮き出るので素早くふき取り、天日干して乾燥させるとクリーム色になります。

**【湿式油抜き】**
　製竹店などでよく行われている方法で「湯晒し」とも呼ばれる方法です。苛性ソーダを入れた熱湯で竹を煮沸し、油分を出します。油分を拭き取った後は、半月〜1カ月ほど天日干しにして乾燥させます。

There are 2 main types of oil extraction; "dry oil extraction" and "wet oil extraction". Wet oil extraction is the way that is used in bamboo stores.

Dry oil extraction

Also called "hisarashi", the bamboo is scorched, making the oil come out. If conducting this process by yourself, you can achieve this by using a gas hob. Place the culm on top of a net and hold it towards the fire until it warms and the oil starts to leak out. Quickly wipe the oil away with a cloth, and leave it to dry in the sun, where it will turn a cream colour.

Wet oil extraction

This is a method that is often used in bamboo stores, and also goes by the name of "yuzarashi". The bamboo is boiled in hot water mixed with sodium hydroxide, which brings out the oil. After wiping the oil away, it should be left to dry in the sun for 1/2 - 1 month.

# 油抜きの工程
Oil extraction process

1  伐採した青竹は水分が多いので、直射日光の当たらない風通しの良い場所で日陰干しにしてから、表面の汚れを取る。

As freshly felled aodake is full of moisture, dry it in the shadows of a well aired room away from direct sunlight, and remove any stains from the surface.

2  晒し加工を行う。苛性ソーダを薄めた熱湯で15分程度、煮沸すると、表面に油分がにじみ出てくる。写真は孟宗竹を釜入れしているところ。向かって右側釜入れ前、左側が釜入後の竹。

Carry out the bleaching process. After boiling the bamboo in sodium hydroxide diluted into hot water for 15 minutes the oil should start to come out. The photograph shows some mosochiku in a pot. On the right is what it looked like before it went in the pot, and on the left is what it looked like after it had been boiled.

3  にじみ出た油分は、ていねいにふき取る。

Carefully wipe away any oil with a cloth.

4  2〜3週間、天日干しにする。干されると、緑色からクリーム色に変化していく。

Dry the bamboo in the sun for 2-3 weeks. When drying it should change from a green to a cream colour.

5  手前が天日干しを終えた晒し竹。出荷まで竹材管理には細心の注意が払われている。

This is bleached bamboo that has finished drying. Much care is paid when handling the bamboo, right up until shipping.

用途に応じ、短くカットされて出荷するものもある。

Some bamboo is cut shorter to purpose and then shipped.

## 油抜きの工程
Oil extraction process

熟練の職人により、質の高い竹材が作られている。
High-quality bamboo is made by skilled craftsmen.

太さや長さ、用途によって選別され出荷を待つ。
The bamboo is sorted by thickness, length, and purpose and waits to be shipped.

[ Chapter 3 ]

# Chapter 4

# 竹ひご作り
Making bamboo strips

「竹かごを作る」と聞いて、
「編む」ことをイメージする人は少なくありません。
けれど、竹かごを手作りしている職人・作家さんたちは、
材料の竹ひごを手作りするところから始めます。
そして、この「竹ひご作り」は、
作品の良し悪しを決めてしまうと言われるほど
重要な工程でもあります。
どのようにして作られるのか、
プロの技を解説を交えて紹介します。

When you hear the phrase "making bamboo baskets",
the image that appears in many people's heads is that of "weaving".
However, craftsmen and artisans
who specialize in making bamboo baskets often start from
the bamboo strip making stage,
which forms the material for their baskets.
This bamboo strip making stage is so important that it is
often said that it will determine
the overall final quality of the basket.
To find out how these strips are made,
we asked the experts.

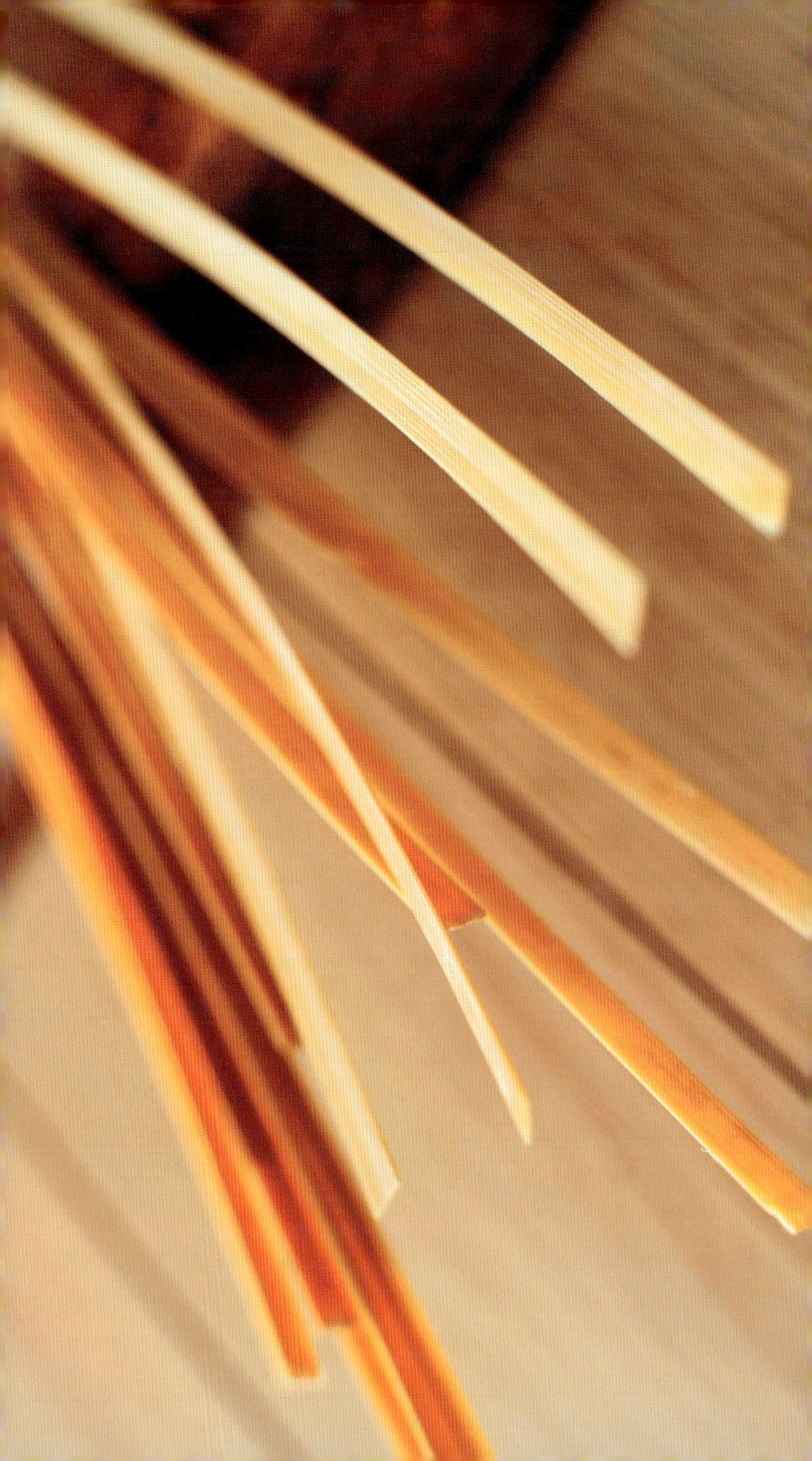

# 竹ひご作りで使う主な道具
The main tools used for making bamboo strips

作りたい物によって、竹ひごの幅、厚み、長さは違ってきます。
写真にあるような道具を使いながら、
幅、厚み、長さなどを調節し、ひご作りをします。

The width, length, and thickness of
the bamboo strips are adjusted depending on
what kind of basket is to be made.
Tools such as these in the photograph are used to do this.

### Ⓐ 幅とり小刀
竹ひごの幅を整えるときと、面とりをするときに使います。

A. Habatori blades
Used to adjust the width of the bamboo strips and cut off any sharp corners.

### Ⓑ けがきコンパス
竹に印をつけるときに使います。

B. Scribe compass
Used for scoring the bamboo.

### Ⓒ 竹割り包丁
竹を割るときに使います。

C. Bamboo-cutting knife
Used for cutting the bamboo.

### D ノギス

竹ひごの厚さや幅を測るとき に使います。

D. Vernier Calipers
Used to measure the width and thickness of the bamboo strips.

### E 裏すき鉎

竹ひごの厚みを均一に整える ときに使います。

E. Urasuk-sen
A tool used to even out the thickness of the bamboo strips.

# 竹ひごを作る
Making the bamboo strips

今回は、幅4mm、厚さ0.5mm、長さ約40cmの竹ひごを作ります。作ってくれるのは竹工芸作家の清水貴之さん。清水さんはプロなので素手で作業していますが、慣れない人がやるとケガをする恐れがありますから必ず軍手を使ってください。

This time we're going to make bamboo strips that are 4mm wide, 0.5mm thick, and 40cm long. The bamboo crasftsman whose going to us how it's done is Takayuki Shimizu. As Shimizu is a professional, he likes to work with his bare hands, but for people who aren't used to this type of work, it is better to wear working gloves to avoid injury.

## STEP 1 ▶ 割る
STEP 1: Cutting

竹ひご作りでは、大まかに「割る」と「剥(は)ぐ」の2つの工程があります。「割る」の工程は、丸い竹を割って竹ひごに近い状態にしていく作業です。「剥ぐ」の工程は、竹の身の部分を取ったり、幅、厚さなどをそろえていく作業です。

The creation of bamboo strips is largely split into 2 steps: "cutting" and "tearing". This is the stage where the round bamboo is cut to create the shape of the bamboo strips.This "shaving" stage is where the softer interior of the bamboo is taken away and the width and thickness of the strips is made uniform.

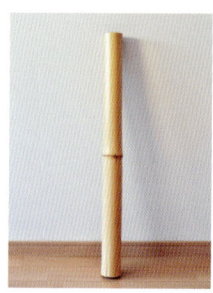

### 【材料】
2、3年物で、直径4cm以上、約80cmの真竹の晒し竹

**Material**
2 or 3 year old bleached madake bamboo that is over 4cm in diameter and around 80cm long.

### ❶ 節刮(ふしく)り
出ている節を落として、面とりのときに引っかからないようにする。刃物と手を固定して竹を回すとやりやすい。

**1. Node removal**
Any bamboo nodes that are sticking out are removed so that the tools don't get caught when the surface is being torn off. This is easiest to accomplish by keeping the blade and your hand in a fixed position and turning the bamboo.

### ❷ ゴミとり
節についているゴミなどを、先がとがっている道具(千枚通しなど)でとる。こうしたちょっとした気配りが、仕上がりを左右する。

**2. Cleaning**
Any dust and dirt is removed from the nodes with a tapered object (such as an awl). This small consideration can have a substantial effect on the final quality of the strips.

❸印をつける

ケガキコンパスを9mmに広げ、竹に9mm間隔で印をつけていく。竹の内側にある2カ所のでっぱりは、枝が生えていたところ。そこからはきれいに半分に割りやすいので、でっぱり部分の外側を起点に印をつける。この竹では20カ所に印がついた。

3. Scoring

A scroll compass is set to a width of 9mm and a mark is scored into the bamboo at 9mm intervals. The 2 protrusions on the inside of the bamboo are the points from which the branches were growing from. Since it is easy to cut the bamboo in half from there, a mark is placed on the outside surface of the protrusion. This piece of bamboo now has 20 marks.

❹割り込み

印をつけたところに竹割り包丁で割り込みを入れていく工程。印に竹割り包丁の刃を入れたら、上からドンドンとたたく。

4. Cutting into the bamboo

This is the stage where a bamboo-cutting knife is used to insert cuts where the bamboo is scored. Once the blade of the bamboo splitting knife goes in, it is hammered down from the top.

❺荒割り（1）

割り込みを入れたところを全て割っていく工程。まずは丸い竹の半分の位置にある割り込みに竹割り包丁の刃を入れて、半分に割る（半分に割る作業を半割りという）。

5. Arawari (1)

This is the stage where the incisions in the bamboo are fully split. Firstly, the blade of the knife is inserted into the incision along the halfway point of the round bamboo, and the bamboo is split in half. (The step where the bamboo is split in half is called "hanwari".)

❻荒割り（2）

半分に割った竹を、さらに半分に割っていく。人の手による作業なので、割る際には正確に半分にはならない。少ない方を自分の身体に向けて割るようにするのがポイント。

6. Arawari (2)

The split-in-half bamboo is then split in half again. Since this work is done by hand, the bamboo isn't cut precisely halfway. The trick is to turn the smaller piece towards your body then cut.

❼荒割り（3）

節は危ないので落とす。

7. Arawari (3)

The nodes can be dangerous, so they are cut off.

❽荒割り（4）

作業を繰り返し、写真のように細くしていく。

8. Arawari (4)

The cutting in half process is repeated until the strips are as thin as in this photograph.

❾荒割り（5）

枝が入っている箇所は割れないので使わない。

9. Arawari (5)

Since the points where the branches joined onto the bamboo cannot be cut, they are not used.

荒割り完了。

This is the end of the arawari stage.

# STEP 2 ▶ 剥ぐ
## STEP 2: Tearing

### ⑩ 荒剥(あらは)ぎ(1)
皮と身を剥ぐ工程。皮と身の比率が3:7を目安に剥ぐ。剥ぐときは、最初だけ竹割り包丁の刃を入れる。

10. Arahagi (1)
This is the step where the bark and the bamboo interior are torn into a 3:7 ratio. When tearing the wood, you only insert the blade of bamboo-cutting knife at the beginning.

### ⑪ 荒剥ぎ(2)
刃で皮と身に少し剥がれたら、写真のように竹割り包丁の胴金の部分を使うと、作業しやすいし危なくない。

11. Arahagi (2)
When you've torn the bark and interior slightly, you can use the middle of the bamboo-cutting knife to complete this step easily and safely, as shown in the photograph.

### ⑫ 荒剥ぎ(3)
節のところは竹割り包丁が進みにくいので、一方の手で竹をしっかり押さえて節を越えていく。その際、節をこえたところが薄くならないように気をつける。

12. Arahagi (3)
It's very difficult to pass the knife through the nodes, so the bamboo needs to be pressed down with one hand and the knife forced through. Make sure that the area above the node doesn't become any thinner.

荒剥ぎを終えた状態。均一に剥けていれば、曲げるときにきれいな円にできる。

This is how the bamboo strips look after they've been roughly torn. Once they've been torn uniformly, they'll form a perfect circle when bent.

### ⑬ 小割(こわ)り(1)
身から剥いだ皮を半分に割る工程(中割りと言う人もいる)。このときは竹割り包丁の刃の部分を使う。

13. Kowari (1)
This is the stage where you cut the bark that you torn away from the bamboo interior in half (some people also call this stage "nakawari"). We use the blade of the bamboo-cutting knife for this stage.

### ⑭ 小割り(2)
節のところは竹割り包丁が進みにくいので、一方の手で竹をしっかり押さえて刃を入れ、節を越えていく。

14. Kowari (2)
It's very difficult to pass the knife through the nodes, so the bamboo needs to be pressed down with one hand and the knife forced through.

#### ⑮小割り(3)
割っているとき、均等にならず一方が細くなることもある。その場合は細くなった方に刃先を向けて割っていくと修正できる。

15. Kowari (3)
When cutting there are times when the pieces don't cut to exactly the same size and one piece becomes narrower. To fix this, direct the tip of the blade towards the narrower side and cut.

#### ⑯薄剥(うすは)ぎ(1)
厚さ0.5mmに近づけていく工程。ケガ防止のため、親指と人差し指にテープを巻いてから作業に入る。

16. Usuhagi (1)
This step will allow us to get closer to that 0.5mm thickness that we want. To prevent injury, this step should be carried out after wrapping tape around your thumb and index finger.

#### ⑰薄剥ぎ(2)
竹割り包丁を使って小割りした竹を薄く剥ぎ、厚さ0.5mmに近づける。

17. Usuhagi (2)
Use a bamboo-cutting knife to thinly tear the thinly cut bamboo until the thickness approaches 0.5mm.

#### ⑱薄剥ぎ(3)
節のところは、力を強め刃先をぐっと入れて節を越えていく。

18. Usuhagi (3)
For the nodes, put more force into the tip of the blade as you cut your way through.

荒剥ぎと薄剥ぎを終えたもの。
Roughly and thinly torn bamboo.

# STEP 3 ▸ 仕上げ
STEP 3: The finish

### ⑲ 水につける
水につけて竹をやわらかくする。目安は10〜15分。水につけると少し色が濃くなる。写真の右は水につけたばかりのもの、左は15分以上つけたもの。

19. Soak in water
Soak the bamboo in water to soften it up for approximately 10-15 minutes. The colour will also become darker. The bamboo on the right has just been submerged in water, while that on the left has been left to soak for over 15 minutes.

### ⑳ 幅とり（1）
幅をそろえる工程。木の台に2本の幅とり小刀を5.5mmの間隔で、木づちなどを使って打ちこむ。その際、刃の角度が同じになるようにする。

20. Habatori (1)
This step will make the width of the strips uniform. Use a wooden mallet to hammer 2 habatori blades into a block of wood 5.5mm apart. Make sure that the blades are positioned at the same angle.

### ㉑ 幅とり（2）
竹の皮を下にして引き、ひっくり返して持っていたところも引く。その際、竹の棒などで竹を押さえるとずれずに引きやすい。幅とりでは、引いたときに出る余分な竹が左右均等になるのが理想。

21. Habatori (2)
Place the bamboo with the bark facing down into the gap and pull it through. Then turn it over and pull through the area that you were holding as well. If you press down the bamboo firmly with a bamboo rod it should slide through easily without slipping. When taking off the width, it is ideal if the amount of excess bamboo coming off both sides is about the same.

### ㉒ 面とり（1）
竹の面をとる工程。面とりをすると引っかかりがなくなって手触りがよくなるし、見た目もより美しくなる。まずは準備として、木の台に幅とり小刀を木づちなどを使って打ちこむ。その際、刃の斜めの部分が、自分側になるように打ちこむ。

22. Mentori (1)
This stage takes away the sharp corners of the bamboo. By taking away the corners of the bamboo, you take away any sharp spots that could get caught, make the bamboo feel smoother, and improve its appearance. Firstly, use a wooden mallet to hammer 2 habatori knives into a wooden block in preparation. Make sure to hammer the blades in so that the slanted part of the blade is on your side.

**㉓ 面とり(2)**
竹の元(竹が生えていた下の方)から引く。その際、竹の棒などで竹を押さえるとずれずに引きやすい。特に節を通すときは、浮き上がらないようにしっかり押さえる。

23. Mentori (2)
Pull the bamboo from its base (where it was growing from). If you press down on the bamboo with a bamboo rod it should slide through easily without slipping. When cutting through the nodes especially, press the rod down firmly so that the bamboo doesn't slip upwards.

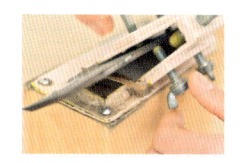

**㉔ 裏すき(1)**
厚さを均一に、そしてきれいに整えるための工程。まず裏すき銑(せん)の台に裏隙銑をセット。そして、今回は厚さ0.5mmのひごを作るので、裏隙銑と刃と台の隙間は0.5mmに合わせる。

24. Urasuki (1)
This stage evens out the thickness and makes the bamboo strips perfectly uniform. Firstly, set an urasukisen on a urasukisen board. Since we are going to make strips that are 0.5mm thick this time, set the space between the urasukisen, blade, and board to 0.5mm.

**㉕ 裏すき(2)**
台と裏隙銑の隙間にひごを入れて引く。

25. Urasuki (2)
Pull the strips through the space between the urasukisen and the board.

**㉖ 裏すき(3)**
節のところは隙間を通らないので、写真のように隙間から外して引く。

26. Urasuki (3)
Since the nodes will not fit through the gap, remove the bamboo strip from the gap and pull like in the photograph.

完成した竹ひご。
The finished bamboo strips.

## Chapter 5

# 編組（編み方）の種類
### Types of weaves (weaving techniques)

竹工芸の編み方は「編組」と呼ばれ、
竹かごは編組品とも言われています。
基本の編組には「四つ目編み」「六つ目編み」
「網代編み」「ござ目編み」「八つ目編み」などがありますが、
基本の編組から派生した編組（例えば「六つ目編み」から
派生した「麻の葉編み」）が多様にあります。
これらの編組を組み合わせると、
200種類以上の編み方が可能だとも言われています。

The weaving techniques of bamboo crafts are called "henso"
and bamboo baskets are also called "hensohin" (products of henso).
Among the basic weaving techniques are
the "yotsume weave", "mutsume weave", "ajiro weave",
"gozame waeve", and the "yatsume weave",
as well as a multitude of derivative weaves
(such as the "asanoha weave",
which is derived from the mutsume weave.)
When combined, it's said that you can use these techniques
to create over 200 types of weave.

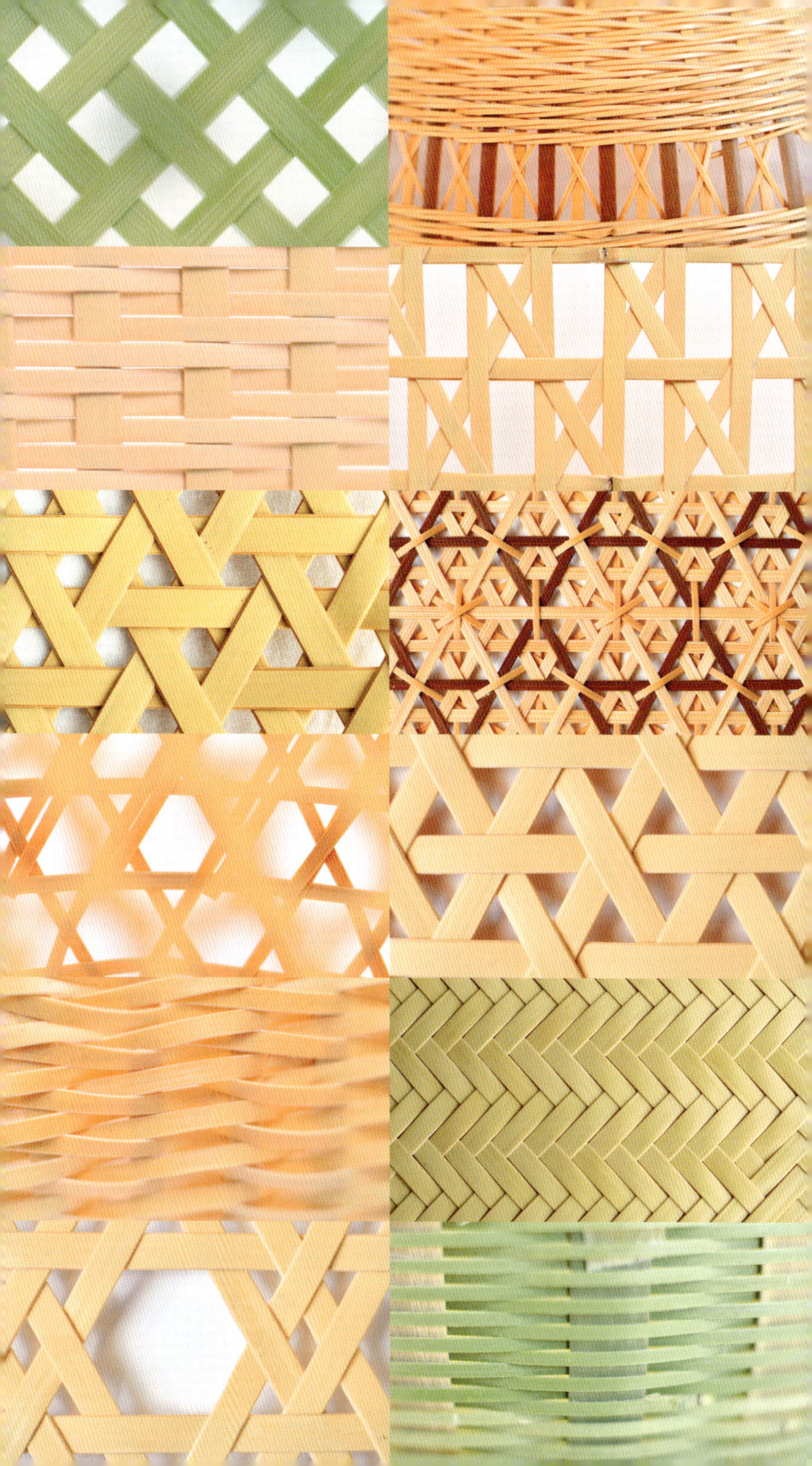

## 胴編み  Basket trunk weaves

オーソドックスな編組には「四つ目編み」「六つ目編み」「網代編み」「ござ目編み」があります。また、数は少ないですが「八つ目編み」も基本的な編み方のひとつです。

The orthodox weaving styles are the "yotsume weave", "mutsume weave", "ajiro weave", and the "gozame weave". Though it's rarer, the "yatsume weave" is also regarded as a basic weave.

### 【四つ目編み系】
Types of yotsume weave (also known as "cross weave")

#### 四つ目編み
基本中の基本と言われている編み方で、縦横の竹ひごを平行に組んで正方形を作ります。平行する竹ひごの間隔を等しく編むのがポイントです。

Yotsume weave
Called the most basic of basic weaves, this is a square-weave style where the horizontal and vertical strips are woven concurrently. The trick to this style is to make the spaces between the interwoven strips equal.

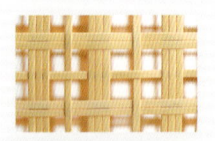

四つ目編みで、平行するひごを2本一組、3本一組にアレンジしたもの。こうした工夫で、違った表情のかごを作ることもできます。

These strips have been woven concurrently in groups of 2 and 3. You can come up with a few different yotsume weave looks through this step.

#### 菱四つ目編み
一般的な四つ目編みは縦横のひごを直角に交差させますが、やや斜めに交差させて編むと編み目がひし形になります。

Hishi yotsume weave
The normal yotsume weave is created by criss-crossing the horizontal and vertical strips perpendicularly, but this hishi yotsume technique is woven at a partial slant, resulting in a diamond pattern.

#### 差し四つ目編み
四つ目の編み目に対し、対角線になるように交差したひごが通っていることから「差し四つ目編み」と呼ばれますが、「四つ目崩し編み」とも言われています。

Sashi yotsume weave
Compared to the stitches in the yotsume weave, the stitches in the sashi yotsume weave are crisscrossed into diagonal lines, giving it the "yotsume kuzushi weave" name, as well as the "sashi yotsume weave" title.

（左）差し四つ目編みをベースに、斜めに片方だけ差す編み方で編んだもの。

A weave woven diagonally one way through a sashi yotsume weave base.

### 【八つ目編み系】
Types of Yatsume weave (also known as "octagonal weave")

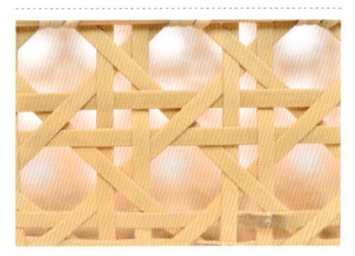

#### 八つ目編み
編み目が八角形なので「八つ目編み」と呼ばれていますが、小さな四つ目もある複雑なデザインは、かごバッグなどの"見せるかご"に好まれます。

Yatsume weave
As the stitches in this weave form octagons, it is named the "yatsume weave", but some designs contain intricate square patterns too, making them preferable for display baskets such as basket bags.

100

## 【網代編み系】

Types of ajiro weave (also known as "netting weave")

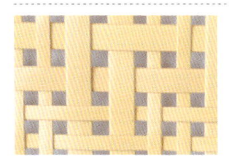

### 二本とび網代編み

とび数や、ひごをすくう数の変化で模様を表せるなど、バリエーションが多いのが網代編みの特徴でもあります。2本飛ばしで編むのが「二本とび網代編み」です。

Nihontobi ajiro weave
What stands out about ajiro weaves is that there are so many variations that change depending on the number of strips woven under and how many other perpendicular strips they miss. Weaves where 2 strips are missed out together are known as "nihontobi ajiro weaves".

### 三本とび網代編み

3本とばしで編む「3本とび網代編み」では、びっちりと目が詰まった編み目ができます。昔は、行李や弁当箱などによく使われていました。

Sanbontobi ajiro weave
Woven by missing 3 perpendicular strips. With the stitches of the sanbontobi ajiro weave, you can close the stitches snugly. In the past it was often used for luggage and bento lunchboxes.

### 桝網代編み

中心がはっきりしており、周囲に向かって桝目が広がっていく編目です。

Masu ajiro weave
While the center of the weave is defined, the grid pattern becomes looser towards the edges.

### 連続桝網代編み

「三本とび網代編み」から派生した編み方で、文庫や盛りかごなどに見られます。

Renzoku masu ajiro weave
This is a weave derived from the sanbontobi ajiro weave, and is often found used in book and morikago baskets.

### 透かし網代編み

「透かし網代編み」は、竹の涼しさを楽しめる編組です。東北地方のすず竹細工では、透かし網代編みのかごバッグがよく見られます。

Sukashi ajiro weave
The sukashi ajiro weaves is a weave type that allows you to enjoy the breeziness of bamboo. You often see sukashi ajiro woven basket bags in the Tohoku region's suzu take bamboo works.

## 【その他】

Others

### やたら編み

不規則に編む技法で、編み目を隠しながら隙間を埋めていきます。「みだれ編み」とも呼びます。

Yatara weave
This is an irregular technique where the stitches are hidden and any gaps are covered up. It's also called the "midare weave".

胴編み  Basket trunk weaves

## 【ござ目編み系】
Types of gozame weave (also known as "mat weave")

### ござ目編み
ざるなどの日用品によく使われたことから「ざる目編み」と言われます。網代編みが織物で言う綾織りだとすれば、ござ目編みは平織りです。

Gozame weave
Since it's often used for everyday items such as zaru plates, this weave technique is also known as the "zarume weave". If you were to compare them to woven fabrics, the ajiro weave would be a twill weave, and the gozame weave would be a plain weave.

### 二本とびござ目編み
2本とばしで編んでいくものを「2本とびござ目編み」と呼びます。

Nihontobi gozame weave
When 2 strips of bamboo are missed at a time, it's called the "nihontobi gozame weave".

### 山路編み
横に回っているひごの模様が、山の路を斜めに登っているように見えることから、この名がついたと言われています。

Yamaji weave
It's said that this name was invented because the pattern of the bamboo strips that lie horizontally slant their way upwards like a mountain road.

## 【縄目編み系】
Types of nawame weave

### 青海編み
波を扇形に描き表す文様のことを青海波と言うところから、「青海波編み」とも呼ばれます。

Seikai weave
The wave-like design of this pattern is like a blue ocean wave, giving this weave the alternative name of the "Seigaiha" (blue ocean wave).

### 松葉編み
編み方は青海編みと同じですが、一周してきたときに縦の骨ひごを1本よけいにとばして、3本とばしを1回してから2本とびを繰り返すと「松葉編み」になります。

Matsuba weave (also known as "pine needle pattern")
Though this weave is the same as the seikai weave, once you have gone around the basket once, miss out an extra vertical piece of bamboo on the frame. Then repeat a pattern of missing 3 strips, then missing 2 to get the matsuba weave.

### 三本縄目編み
「ござ目編み」、「松葉編み」、「青海編み」などで花籠を編む際の立ち上がりや、最後の編みどめなどによく使われます。

Sanbon nawame weave
Often used to build up or end flower baskets woven in gozame, matsuba, or seikai weaves.

## 【六つ目編み系】
Types of mutsume weave (also known as "hexagonal weave")

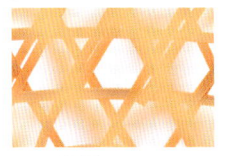

### 六つ目編み
六角形の編み目が印象的ですが、斜めの構成でできた強度のある編み方でもあります。古くは正倉院の御物にも「六つ目編み」を用いたものがあるなど、幅広い用途のかごに使われてきました。

Mutsume weave
Though the hexagonal stitches are impressive, it is also a strong weave made from a diagonal structure. In the past, the mutsume weave technique was used for baskets with multiple purposes and was even used for some imperial treasures that were kept at the Shosoin storehouse.

### 二重六つ目編み
六つ目編みの各辺が、二重になっている編組です。

Niju mutsume weave
A weave where each round of mutsume weaving is doubled up.

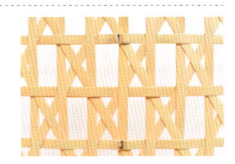

### 差し六つ目編み
六つ目を編んで編み地にひごを差していきます。しゃれた印象を活かし、花籠、かごバッグなどに使われています。

Sashi mutsume weave
A mutsume weave is woven and then bamboo strips incorporated into it. Lending the basket a stylish feel, this weave is often used for flower baskets and basket bags.

### 六つ目菊編み
着色のひごで一回り大きい六つ目を編み重ね、さらに細いひごで縫い合わせていきます。

Mutsume kiku weave
Thick rounds of large mutsume weave are woven which are then sewn together with thinner strips of bamboo.

### 麻の葉編み
六つ目編みから派生した編組の中では、よく見られる編み方です。「麻の葉編み」からさらに派生した「麻の葉つぶし」「麻の葉崩し」という編み方もあります。

Asanoha weave
This is an often seen derivative of the mutsume weave. There are also weaves called the "asanoha tsubushi" and "asanoha kuzushi", which have been derived from the asanoha weave itself.

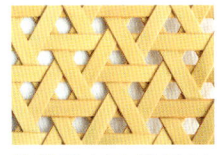

### 鉄線編み（亀甲編み）
6本のひごが交わる交点を組まず、中心に寄せると小さな六角形ができます。この編み目がクレマチスの花に似ていることから、クレマチスの別名「鉄線」にちなんだ名で呼ばれるようになりました。

Tessen weave (Kikko weave)
Without connecting the 6 bamboo strips at the intersect and by directing them towards the middle, you can make a small hexagonal pattern. As these stitches resemble a clematis flower, this weave was named "tessen", which is another name for the clematis.

# 底編み　Base weaves

種類は胴編みほど多くはなく、四角形のかごでは四つ目底や四つ目筏（いかだ）底、円形のかごでは菊底が見られます。

Though there aren't as many types of base weaves as there are trunk weaves, yotsume base and yotsume ikada base can often be found in square baskets, and the kiku base in round baskets.

## 【四つ目編み系】
Types of yotsume weaves

### 四つ目底
その名の通り、四つ目編みで編んだ底のことです。胴編みは四つ目編みに限定されるわけではなく、四つ目底からござ目編みでおこしていくかごなどがあります。

**Yotsume base**
As the name suggests, this is a base woven with the yotsume weave. The trunk weave on top is not limited to a yotsume weave only, and there are some baskets that start from a yotsume base and move onto a gozame weave further up.

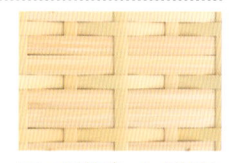

### 四つ目筏（いかだ）底
四つ目の間に幅広のひごを差しこんだ様子が筏のように見えることから、この名で呼ばれています。四角形の底面を平らに加工できる底編みとして、広く使われています。

**Yotsume ikada base**
As thicker bamboo strips are interwoven into the yotsume weave, the pattern resembles a raft (ikada), which is where this weave gets its name from. This is often used as a weave to provide a flat and rectangular base.

## 【ござ目編み系】
Types of gozame weave

### 菊底
菊の花のような形をしていることから、この名がつきました。幅の広い骨ひごを中心で交差させて、細いひご2本でござ目編みで編んでいきます。円形のかごのふたなどにも使われます。

**Kiku base (also known as "chrysanthemum base weave")**
This weave gets its name from its chrysanthemum (kiku) patterning. Wide bamboo frame strips are intersected and 2 thinner strips of bamboo are incorporated into the design through a gozame weave. It's also often used as a lid for round baskets.

## 【輪弧編み系】
Types of rinko weave (also known as "bull's eye weave")

### 輪弧底
中央に輪ができる底編みで、別府で生まれた盛りかごの「鉄鉢」が有名です。

**Rinko base**
This is a base weave that leaves an empty ring in the center. The "teppachi" morikago basket from Beppu is particularly famous.

## 【網代編み系】
Types of ajiro weaves

### 四方網代底
網代底で正方形のかごを作るときに、よくある編み方です。

**Shiho ajiro base**
This is a weave that's often used when making an ajiro weave base for a square basket.

# 縁作り Fuchizukuri (rim making)

かご作りの仕上げは、縁作りです。大きくは「巻縁」と「当縁」の2種類があり、そこから派生した技法が多様にあります。
One of the finishing touches of basket weaving is fuchizukuri. Broadly speaking it is split into 2 types, "makibuchi" and "atebuchi", with a multitude of techniques derived from each.

## 【巻縁系】
Types of makibuchi

### 巻縁(まきぶち)
かご本体の縁部分に芯になる竹をそえてから、編んできたひごとともに別のひごを巻いて仕上げます。

Makibuchi
After drawing in the bamboo strips that make up the frame towards the edge, a separate bamboo strip is wrapped around them together with woven strips to create a rim.

## 【当縁系】
Types of atebuchi

### 当縁(あてぶち)
かご本体の縁部分に厚めのひごを当て、編んできたひごを挟んでから、ところどころを縛って固定させる技法です。

Atebuchi
A thick bamboo strip is attached to the edge of the basket and ran through the woven strips, where it is tied in certain places to secure it down.

### 柾割(まさわり)当縁
別府竹細工では、平ざるの縁仕上げに使われることがよくあります。

Masawari atebuchi
Often used to make the edges of flat zaru dishes in Beppu bamboo work.

## 【共縁系】
Types of tomobuchi

### 共縁(ともぶち)
編みひごをそのまま、縁仕上げに使う方法です。

Tomobuchi
A technique for creating an edge that uses the bamboo strips as they are.

### えび止め
共縁仕上げのひとつに「えび止め」があります。

Ebidome
"Ebidome" is a type of tomobuchi finish.

## Chapter 6

# 編み方
### How to weave

基本的な編み方の「四つ目編み」と「六つ目編み」で
竹かごを作る工程を紹介します。
基本中の基本と言われる「四つ目編み」は、
古くから農具・漁具や生活用品、建築などに
幅広く使われる一方で、
「市松」とも評されるシンプルな格子柄は、
モダンな編み方として好まれています。
また、「六つ目編み」と言えば六角形の目が特徴的ですが、
この六角形がきれいになるように編んでいくのが
ポイントでもあります。

Here we will introduce the basic weaving techniques;
the "yotsume weave" and the "mutsume weave".
Said to be the most basic of basic weaves,
the yotsume weave has been used for a long time for
a range of things, including farming and fishing tools,
as well as everyday wares and construction,
and forms a simple check pattern named "ichimatsu",
that is well-liked as a more modern weaving style.
The mutsume weave is characterized by
its hexagonal stitches, and the trick is to pay attention into
forming the hexagonal shapes neatly.

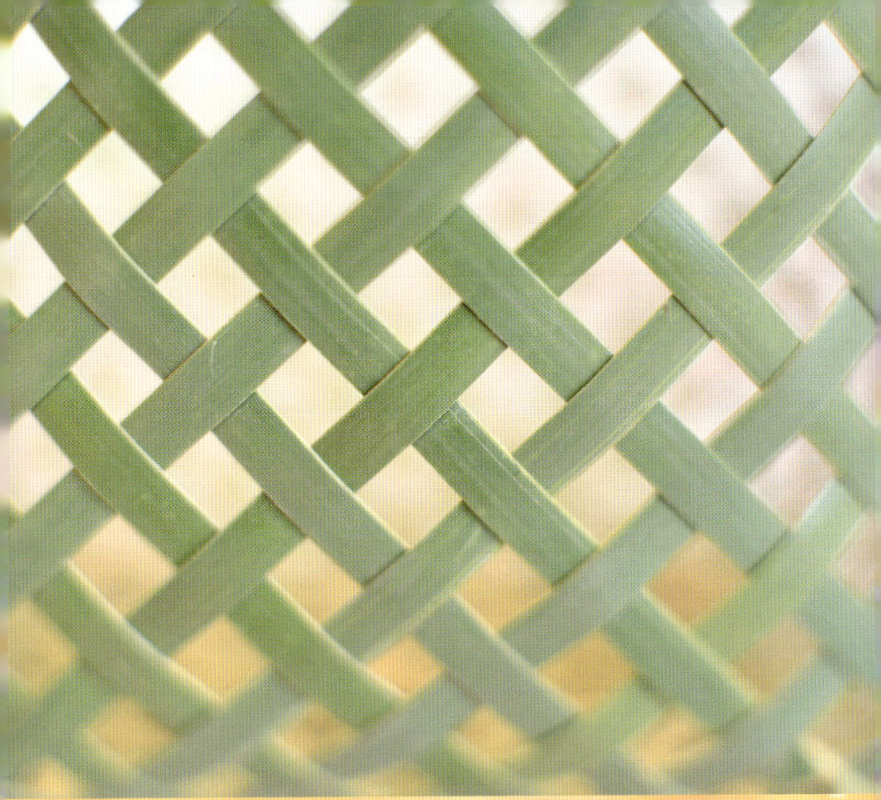

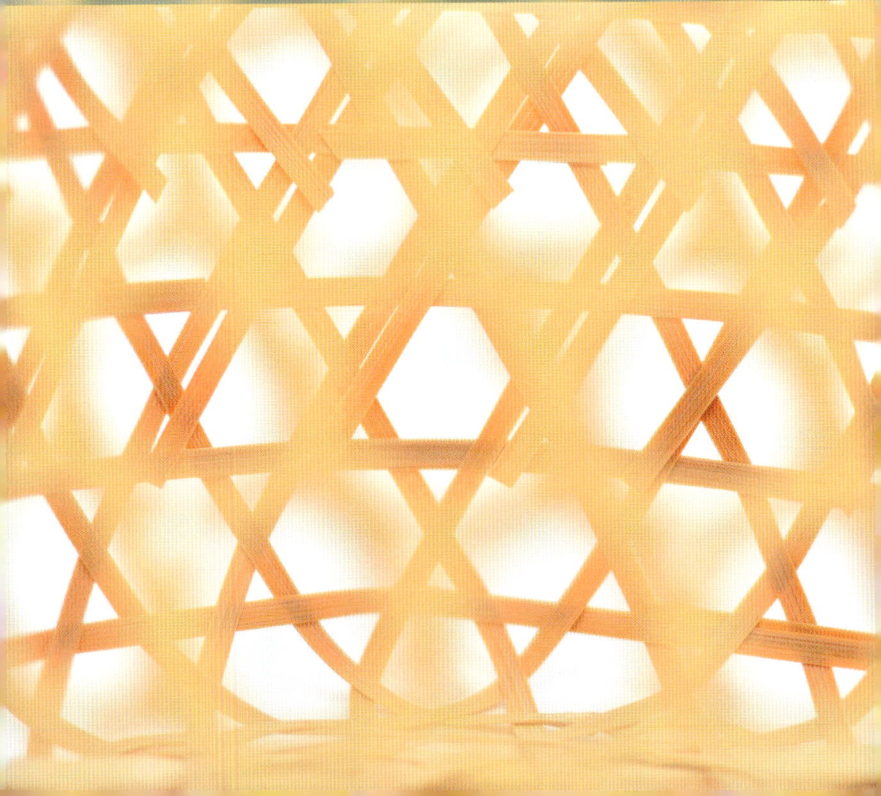

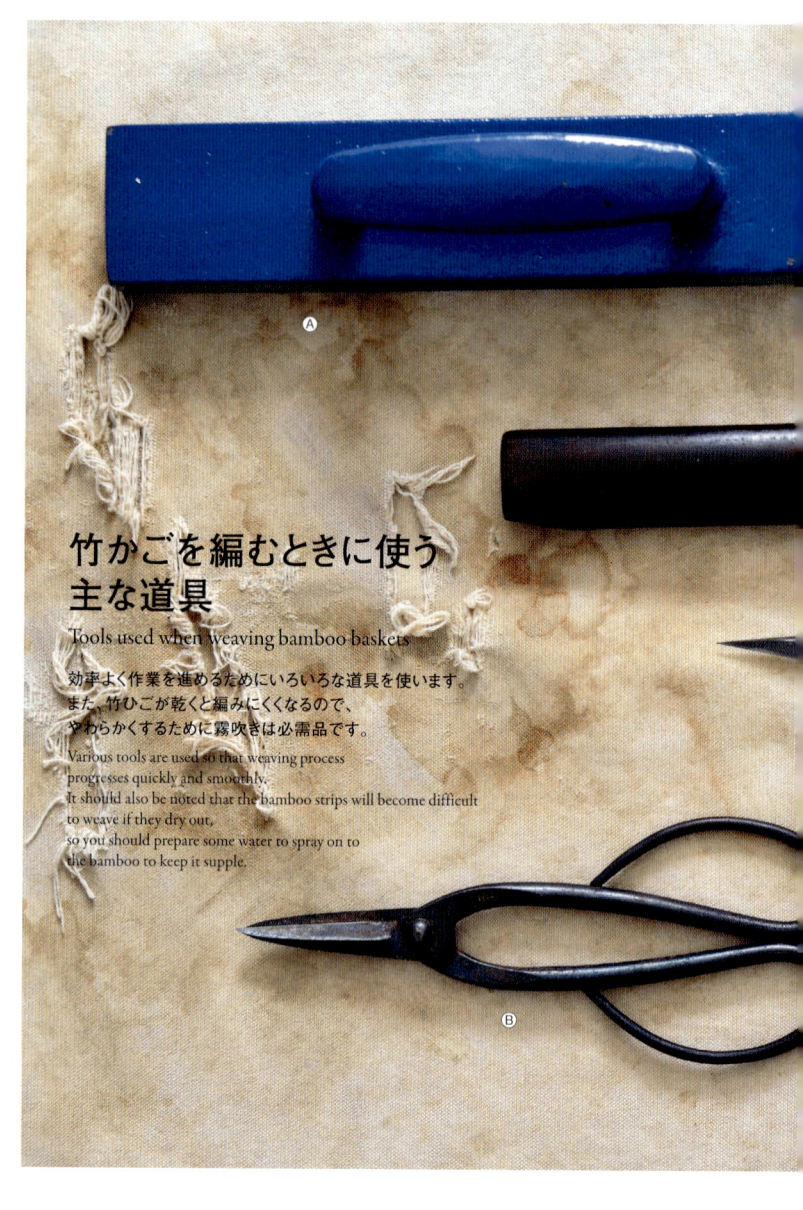

## 竹かごを編むときに使う主な道具
Tools used when weaving bamboo baskets

効率よく作業を進めるためにいろいろな道具を使います。
また、竹ひごが乾くと編みにくくなるので、
やわらかくするために霧吹きは必需品です。

Various tools are used so that weaving process
progresses quickly and smoothly.
It should also be noted that the bamboo strips will become difficult
to weave if they dry out,
so you should prepare some water to spray on to
the bamboo to keep it supple.

### Ⓐ 文鎮
編み地がずれないように重石になるものを置きます。

A. Paperweight
A stone object is placed on the basket so that it doesn't slip.

### Ⓑ 剪定バサミ
竹ひごをカットするときなどに使います。

B. Pruning shears
For tearing the bamboo strips etc.

### Ⓒ 小刀
縁用の竹などを削るときに使います。

C. A small knife
For tearing the bamboo for the rim.

### Ⓓ 仮止め用の身竹

編んだところがバラバラにならないよう、仮止めをするときなどに使います。

D. Bamboo stopper
Used to prevent the bamboo strips from coming apart from each other and creating temporary stops.

### Ⓔ 千枚通し

細いひごを狭い隙間に通すときに便利です。

E. Awl
Useful for threading thin bamboo strips through tight spaces.

### Ⓕ くじり

編み目をそろえたり広げたりするときに使います。

F. Kujiri
Used to adjust and widen the stitches etc.

# 四つ目編みのかご

A yotsume weave basket

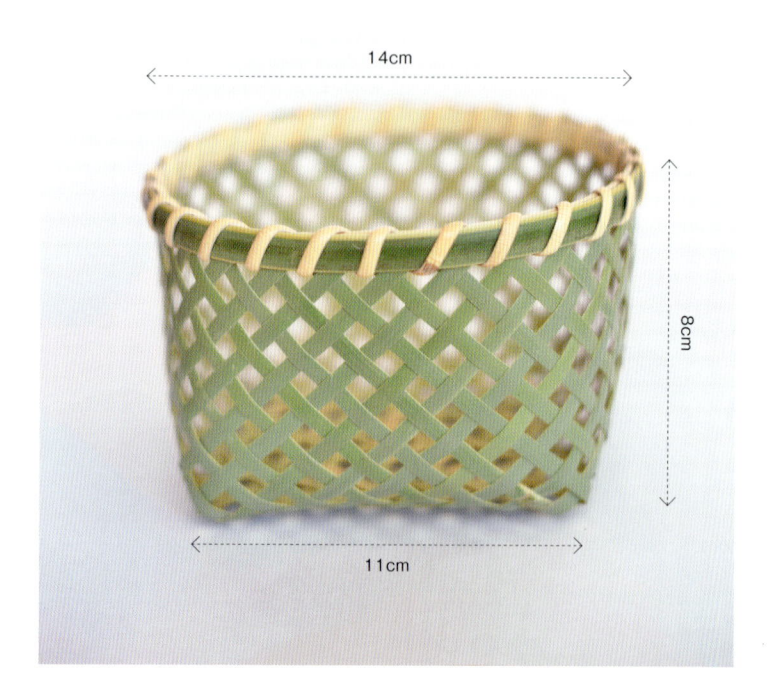

**【材料】**
幅5mm、厚さ0.6mm、長さ(真ん中に節がある状態で)50cmの竹ひご×28本 ※長方形のかごにも応用できるように、正方形にしては長めのひごを用意した。／幅9mmの縁作りに使う竹／幅4mmの巻籐×1本

Materials
28 x 5mm wide, 0.6mm thick, and 50cm long (with nodes still intact in the middle) bamboo strips *Longer strips were prepared to make them suitable for rectangular and square baskets. / 9mm wide bamboo strips for the rim. / 1 x 4mm wide makifuji strip

**【道具】**
竹ひごを作ったときに出る身竹(仮止め用)／長さ14cmの仮力竹×2本／木工ボンド／竹割包丁／クリップ／鉛筆／剪定バサミ／霧吹き／千枚通し

Tools
The interior of the bamboo from the strip making stage (to make a stopper) / 2 x 14cm long temporary bamboo support strips / Wood glue / Bamboo-cutting knife / Clips / Pencil / Pruning shears / Spray / Awl

竹の縁を籐で巻いた「流し巻き」。籐の白さがアクセントにもなっている。

This is a "nagashimaki", where a cane has been wrapped around the basket rim. The whiteness of the cane provides a nice accent to the design.

底を四つ目編みで編み、底編みのひごでそのまま立ち上げている。

These simple checked stitches look beautiful once their height, width, levelness, and perpendicularity have been fixed.

竹工芸作家の
勢司恵美さん。

Bamboo craaftswoman
Emi Seishi

縦・横・水平・垂直が整っているのが美しい、格子柄のシンプルな編目。

The base is woven with the yotsume weave and built upwards from the base strips.

## STEP 1 ▸ 底を編む
### STEP 1: Weaving the base

### 1段目を編む  Weaving the first level

❶5mm幅のひごを5mm間隔で、四つ目編みで14㎝四方の底を編んでいく。1本目は板の赤丸の上に節がくるようにおく。四つ目編みでは「おさえる・すくう」の交互に編む。また、節は節を上にのせて編むようにするのがポイント。

1. Using 5mm wide strips of bamboo set 5mm apart, use the yotsume weave to weave a base that measures 14cm on all sides. Take the first strip and position it so that the node lines up with the red circle on the board. Use the yotsume weave to weave over and under alternately. Try to make it so that the node of one strip ends up on top of the node of the other.

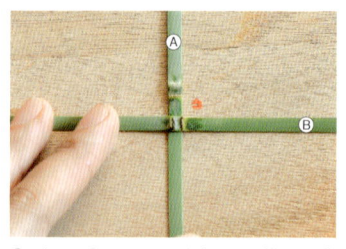

❷2本目はⒶをおさえて、赤丸の下に横おき。Ⓐの上に節がのるようにする。

2. Place the second strip over (A), lying horizontally below the red circle. The node should lay on top of (A) strip.

❸3本目は赤丸の右側にⒷをおさえて縦おき。Ⓑに節がのるようにする。

3. The third strip should lay vertically to the right of the red circle, over (B) strip. Make sure that the node is what lays on top of (B) strip.

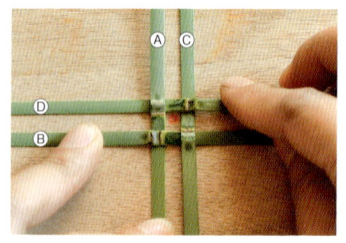

❹4本目はⒸをおさえ、Ⓐをすくい赤丸の上に横おき。節の位置は、Ⓒにのるようにする。ここで小さな四つ目がひとつできた。

4. The fourth strip should lay over (C) but under (A), and should lay horizontally over the red circle. Rest the node over (C) strip. We've made a small yotsume stitch here.

## 2段目から7段目まで編む Weaving levels 2-7

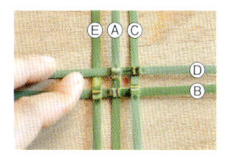

❺2段目以降、左回りに1本ずつひごを足していく。節の位置は、最初の中心の四角を作っている縦の2本か、横の2本の上に節が乗るようにおいていく。5本目はⒹをすくい、Ⓑをおさえる。

5. From the second level onwards, 1 strip needs to be added at a time in a counterclockwise direction. The node of each strip should lay on top of the first 4 strips, whether that be one of the vertical or horizontal strips. The fifth strip should go under (D) but over (B).

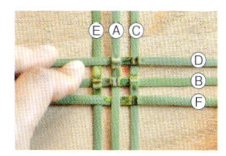

❻6本目は、右から(Ⓒ→Ⓐ→Ⓔ)の順に、おさえる・すくう・おさえる。

6. The sixth strip should weave over → under → over (C → A → E) from the right.

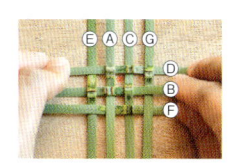

❼7本目は、下から(Ⓕ→Ⓑ→Ⓓ)の順に、おさえる・すくう・おさえる。

7. The seventh strip should weave over → under → over (F → B → D) from the bottom.

❽8本目は、右から(Ⓖ→Ⓒ→Ⓐ→Ⓔ)の順に、おさえる・すくうを繰り返す。

8. The eighth strip should weave over → under → over → under (G → C → A → E) from the right.

❾3段目。9本目は、上から(Ⓗ→Ⓓ→Ⓑ→Ⓕ)の順に、すくう・おさえるを繰り返す。ひごは乾燥すると編みにくくなるので、霧吹きで時々ぬらす(※他のかご作りも同様)。

9. The third level. The ninth strip should repeat under → over in the order (H → D → B → F) from the top. If the strips start to dry out they will be hard to weave so give them a spray of water from time to time. (*This should be done for all baskets.)

113

## STEP 1 ▸ 底を編む　Weaving the base

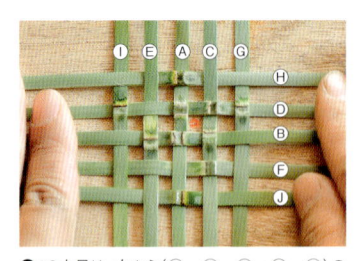

❿10本目は、右から(Ⓖ→Ⓒ→Ⓐ→Ⓔ→Ⓘ)の順に、おさえる・すくうを繰り返す。

10. The tenth strip should repeat over and under in the order (G → C → A → E → I) from the right.

⓫11本目は、下から(Ⓙ→Ⓕ→Ⓑ→Ⓓ→Ⓗ)の順に、おさえる・すくうを繰り返す。

11. The 11th strip should repeat over and under in the order (J → F → B → D → H) from the bottom.

⓬12本目は、右から(Ⓚ→Ⓖ→Ⓒ→Ⓐ→Ⓔ→Ⓘ)の順に、おさえる・すくうを繰り返す。縦6本、横6本で3周分を編み終えた。同じパターンで、残り4周を編んでいく。

12. The 12th strip should repeat over and under in the order (K → G → C → A → E → I) from the right. You've now gone around the weave 3 times and have 6 vertical and 6 horizontal strips. Keep going around and adding strips for a further 4 rotations.

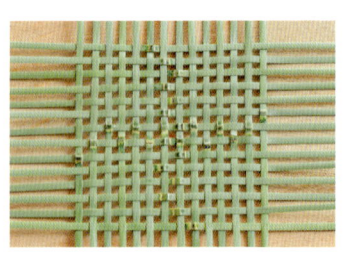

⓭縦14、横14本のひごをすべて使い、7段編んだ状態。これで今回作るかごの底が完成。立ち上がりのところに節があると折れやすくなるので、外側の周の節の位置を写真のようにずらす。

13. You've used up all 14 vertical strips and 14 horizontal strips, going around the weave 7 times by this point. The base for this basket is now complete. If there are any nodes where the strips are build up, they tend to bend very easily, so the nodes on the outer rotation should be shifted to the position shown in the photograph.

## STEP 2 ▸ 胴部分を編む

STEP 2: Weaving the trunk

⓮身竹を今編んでいるひごより薄くして、仮止めのひごを作る。仮止めをしておかないとせっかく編んだ底編みがほどけてバラバラになってしまう。

14. Take a strip of bamboo interior that was discarded during the bamboo strip making stage and make it thinner than the strips that you have been using until now to create a temporary stopper. If you don't do this, the weave that you have just created may come loose and the strips may start to separate.

⓯仮止めは隙間をあけずびったりくっつくぐらいまで入れる。角は折り曲げて仮止めのひごを入れるとなお良い。

15. Fit the stopper snugly around the bottom without leaving a gap. It's even better if you turn the corners up and then fit the stopper.

⓰底に仮止めをしたところ。

16. The base when the temporary stopper has been fitted.

⓱裏側にして、立ち上げる位置に写真のように鉛筆で線を引く。

17. Turn the weave over and draw a line in pencil as shown in the photograph where the strips will begin to stand.

⓲底の長さに合わせて14cmの力竹を2本、先に行くにしたがってとがらせるように作る。力竹は補強用の竹のこと。底面に力竹を入れると、かごの強度を高められるし、"座り"をよくすることもできる。

18. Take two 14cm long strips of bamboo, the same length as your basket base, and tail them off towards the ends. These strips will reinforce and support the basket, and by inserting them into the base you can make the basket stronger and improve its stability.

⓳底側に力竹を写真のように入れる。

19. Insert the bamboo support strips into the base as shown in the photograph.

115

## STEP 2 ▸ 胴部分を編む  Weaving the trunk

⑳編むときに立ち上がりやすくするために、おこしぐせをつける。おこしぐせをつけるときに折れないよう、霧吹きでぬらしてやわらかくする。

20. So that the strips stand up more easily when weaving the trunk, insert a bend into the strips. You don't want the strips to actually fold all the way, so spray them with water to soften them up and prevent a full fold from happening.

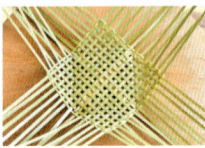

㉑線を引いたところに親指をあて、おこしぐせをつける。

21. Press your thumb against the line you drew, and bend.

㉒力竹の位置を中心に、「右側のひごは左に向かう」「左側のひごは右に向かう」という規則性で、写真のように「おさえる・すくう」のパターンで立ち上げながら編んでいく。

22. Concentrating on the position of the support strips, using "turn the strips on the right towards the left" and "turn the strips on the left towards the right" as a general rule, weave over and under as you build them up, as is shown in the photograph.

㉓編んだところはすぐにはずれてしまうので、クリップや洗濯バサミで固定しておく。

23. The weave can come undone quite quickly, so secure the strips in place with a clip or clothes peg.

㉔「おさえる・すくう」という交互に編むパターンで進んでいく。

24. Continue weaving the strips over and under alternately.

㉕1カ所の角が編みあがったところ。ずれないようにクリップなどで留めておく。

25. This is a finished corner. Secure it with a clip so that it stays in place.

116

㉖編んだところの反対側を、交互に編むパターンで進んでいく。
26. Take the opposite corner and weave in the same way.

㉗4つの角を編み終えたところ。
27. What the basket should look like when you've woven all 4 corners.

㉘仮止めのひごを剪定バサミで切って取り出す。
28. Use the pruning shears to cut out the temporary stopper and remove it.

㉙仮力竹を取る。
29. Remove the temporary bamboo support strips.

㉚立ち上った状態。
30. How the basket looks built up.

117

## STEP 2 ▸ 胴部分を編む  Weaving the trunk

㉛作りたい高さの位置に線を引く。交差しているひごの中心点を結ぶように線を引くと、水平に引くことができる。線が波打ってしまうようなら目がずれているので、線が水平になるように微調整する。

31. Make a mark for however tall that you want the basket to become. By drawing a line that connects the centers of the intersecting strips, you can draw a more level line. If the line becomes too wavy, the stitches will become too off-center, so please make it so that the line is straight and level.

㉜剪定バサミで切る。

32. Cut with pruning shears.

㉝切った状態。

33. How the basket looks cut.

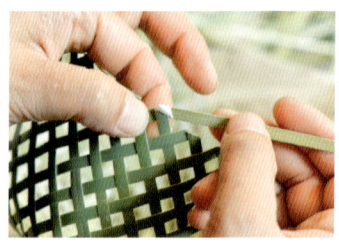

㉞重なっている部分のひごの間に木工ボンドをつけ乾かす。

34. Apply some wood glue between the strips where they over lap and let it dry.

118

## STEP 3 ▸ 縁作り 〜流し巻き〜
STEP 3: Making the rim - Nagashimaki

㉟幅9mmの竹を使う。長さはできあがったかごの円周プラス7cmくらいが目安。竹割包丁で皮と身を剥ぐ。竹の厚みによって変わるが、今回は皮側1.5mm、身側2mmになった。

35. Use strips of bamboo that are 9mm wide. You should aim for a length of the circumference of the finished basket + 7cm. Use a bamboo-cutting knife to tear the bark and interior of the bamboo. Though the thickness may change depending on the bamboo used, this time the bark has been torn to 1.5mm thick and the interior to 2mm thick.

㊱皮と身を剥いだ状態。皮(外縁)は皮側を、身(内縁)は身側を面とりする。

36. How the bamboo looks once the bark and interior have been torn. Do mentori on the bark (outer rim) and bamboo interior (inner rim).

㊲丸めたときに重なる部分(プラス7cmのところ)を合わせと言う。外縁・内縁の両端の合わせの部分、皮側・身側を先がだんだん薄くなるように削り、丸くなるように曲げぐせをつける。

37. The part of the rim that overlaps when it is placed around the top (the +7cm) is called the "awase". Tear both ends of the inner and outer rim so that they gradually get thinner and thinner, and bend a little so that the bamboo forms a circle.

㊳膝を使うと、うまく曲げぐせをつけられる。

38. If you use your knee, you can put this bend in well.

㊴写真のように、外縁を合わせてクリップで留めていく。

39. As shown in the photograph, bring the outer rim together and clip in place.

㊵かごよりも小さめの円を作って内縁をはめる。外縁の合わせとは反対側に合わせがくるように入れ、クリップで留める。

40. Make a circle that's slightly smaller than your basket and attach it to the inner rim. Make sure that the awase is on the opposite side to the awase of the outer rim, and clip in place.

## STEP 3 ▸ 縁作り 〜流し巻き〜 Making the rim - Nagashimaki

❹「流し巻き」という巻き方で籐を巻いていく。籐が手に入らない場合、皮ひもや毛糸などで巻いてもかわいらしく仕上げられる。外縁の合わせの少し右側からスタートする。巻籐の先に木工ボンドつけて、外縁と内縁の間に入れる。

41. Wrap the cane in the "nagashimaki" style. If you can't get hold of any cane, try wrapping some leather or wool instead for a cute finish. Start just at the right of the awase on the outer rim. Apply some wood glue to the end of the cane and insert it between the inner and outer rim.

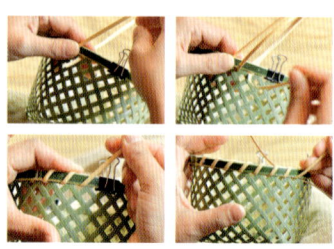

❷ひとつ隣りの穴を通しながら巻いていく。

42. Keep on wrapping it through the next hole in line.

❸合わせのところにきたら木工ボンドをつけてから巻き込む。

43. When you came to the awase, apply some wood glue and keep on wrapping.

❹千枚通しなどをさして浮かせたところに、木工ボンドをつけた巻籐をすべりこませて引っ張る。

44. Poke a tool such as an awl through any places that are sticking up, pass the makifuji, with some wood glue applied, through the gap, and pull.

❺出たところ剪定バサミで切って完成。

45. Cut off what's left sticking out with a pair of pruning shears, and you're done.

Chapter 6

# 六つ目編みのかご
Mutsume weave baskets

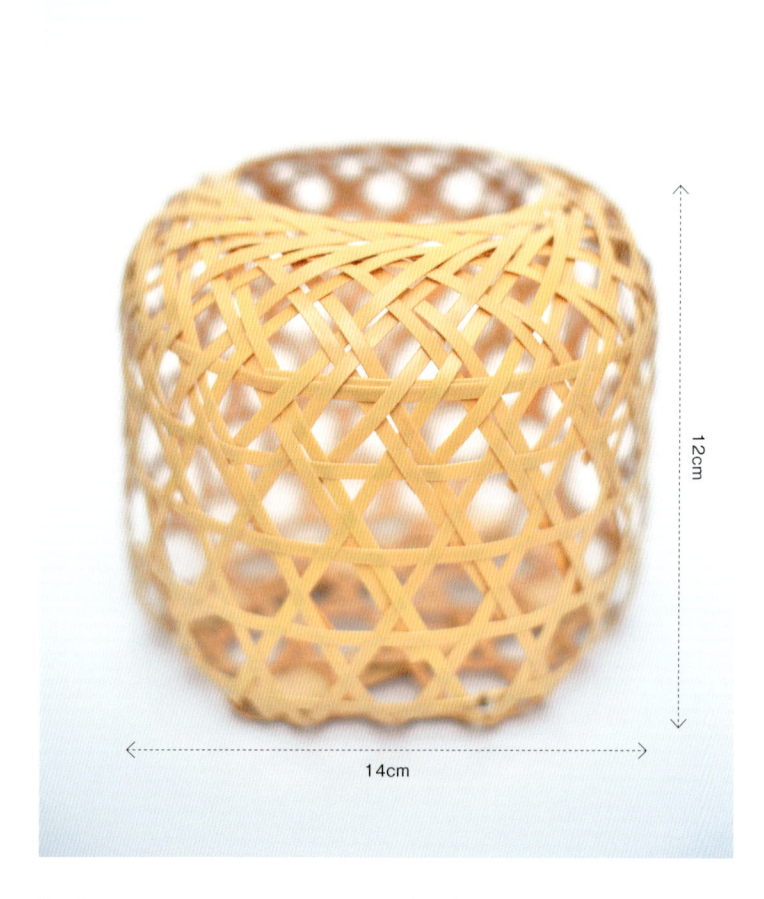

14cm

12cm

【材料】
幅4mm、厚さ0.5mm、長さ約78cmの竹ひご×23本 ※「六つ目編みの編み方」で使う竹ひごは18本／力竹に使う竹

Materials
23 x 4mm wide, 0.5mm thick, approximately 78cm long bamboo strips *18 of these strips will be used for the mutsume weave / Bamboo for support strips

【道具】
60度の線が書いてある板／霧吹き／剪定バサミ／文鎮／身竹で作った仮力竹

Tools
A board with some 60° lines drawn on / Water spray / Pruning shears / Paperweight / A temporary stopper made of bamboo interior

胴編みのひごをそのまま使って縁を作る。

The rim is made from the bamboo strips used to make the trunk.

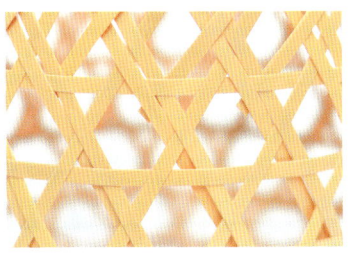

六つ目編みの編目はきれいな六角形で、デザイン性にも富んでいる。それだけに、きれいな六角形になるよう気をつけて編むのがポイントだ。

The stitches of the mutsume weave form beautiful hexagonal patterns which are great for designing. Therefore it's essential that you are careful to make the most beautiful stitches that you can.

8cm

竹工芸作家の
清水貴之さん。

Bamboo craftsman
Takayuki Shimizu

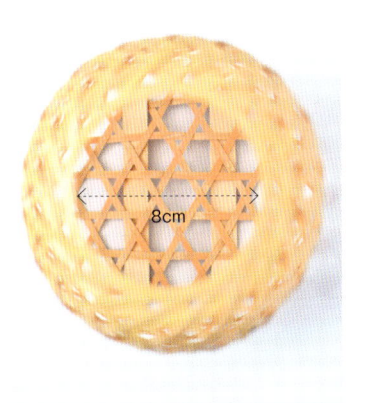

上から見たところ。底も六つ目編みで編んだ「六つ目底」。底面は力竹で補強している。

A view from above. Even the base is woven with a mutsume weave, in this case, the "mutsume base weave". The bottom is reinforced with bamboo.

Chapter 6

# STEP 1 ▶ 底を編む
## STEP 1: Weaving the base

### 1段目（1つ目の六角形）を作る Weaving the first level (making your first hexagonal stitch)

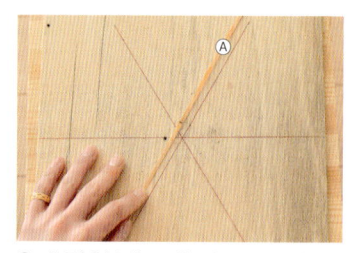

❶1本目（Ⓐ）を斜めの線に合わせて60度におく。60度の線がある板を使えば、線の上に竹ひごをおいていけばいいので、その都度測る手間が省ける。編んでいく際、節は常に上にくるようにする。

1. Place your first strip (A) at a 60° angle going along a diagonal line. If you are using a board with 60° lines drawn onto it, you can place the strips directly on top of the lines without having to measure the angle every time. When weaving, make sure that the nodes always lay on top.

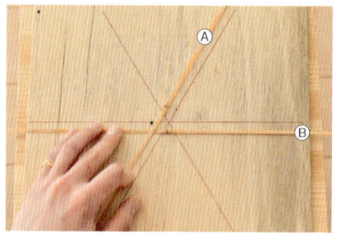

❷2本目（Ⓑ）を横の直線におく。Ⓐをすくう。

2. Place the second strip (B) in a straight horizontal line. Weave it under (A).

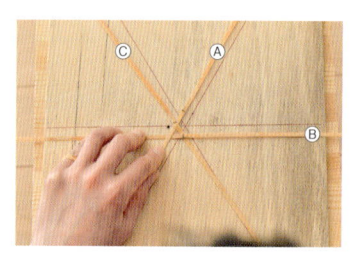

❸3本目（Ⓒ）をⒶと逆側の斜めの線に合わせて60度におく。Ⓐをおさえ、Ⓑをすくう。

3. The third strip (C) should lay on a 60° slant on the opposite side to (A). It should go over (A), but under (B).

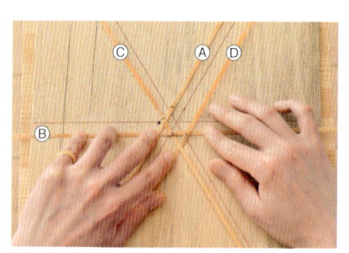

❹4本目（Ⓓ）をⒶと平行に60度におく。Ⓑをおさえ、Ⓒをすくう。

4. Place the fourth strip at a 60° angle parallel to (A). It should go over (B), but under (C).

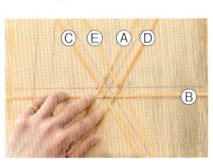

❺5本目(Ⓔ)をⒸと平行に60度におく。Ⓐをすくい、Ⓓをおさえ、Ⓑをすくう。

5. Place the fifth strip (E) at a 60° angel parallel to (C). It should go under (A), over (D), and under (B).

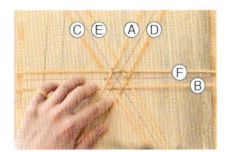

❻6本目(Ⓕ)をⒷと平行におく。Ⓒをおさえ、Ⓐをすくい、Ⓔをおさえ、Ⓓをすくう。

6. The sixth strip (F) should be laid parallel to (B). It should go over (C), under (A), over (E), and under (D).

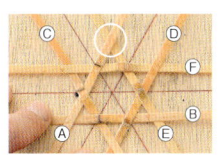

❼ⒶとⒺの白丸印のところを上下組み替える。

7. Rearrange the top and bottom of (A) and (E) where the white circle is.

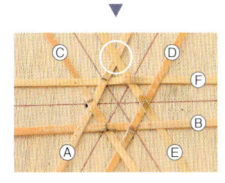

❽組み替えた状態。

8. How it should look rearranged.

❾6カ所に指を入れて縮めると、真ん中がきれいな六角形になる。

9. If you insert your finger into 6 spaces and contract the strips, you'll get a nice hexagon shape.

## STEP 1 ▸ 底を編む　Weaving the base

### 2段目、3段目を編む　Weaving the second and third levels

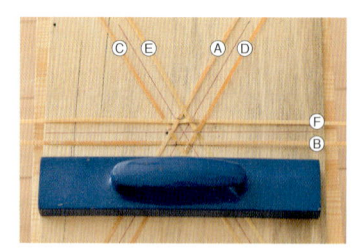

❿手前に文鎮を置いて固定させる。

10. Place the paperweight on the weave in front of you to secure it in place.

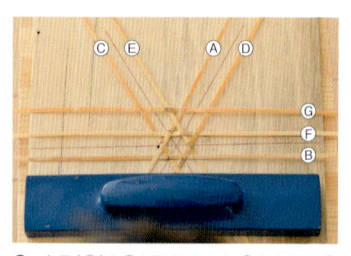

⓫7本目（G）を（F）と平行におく。（C）をすくい、（E）をおさえ、（A）をすくい、（D）をおさえる。

11. Place the seventh strip (G) parallel to (F). Weave it under (C), over (E), under (A), and over (D).

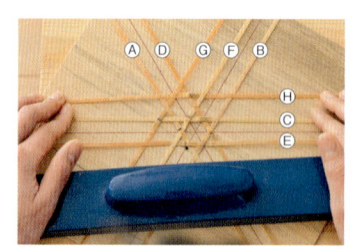

⓬左に60度回転させ、文鎮をおいて固定させる。8本目（H）を（C）と平行におく。（A）をおさえ、（G）をすくい、（D）をおさえ、（F）をすくい、（B）をおさえる。

12. Rotate the weave 60° to the left and secure in place with the paperweight. Place the eighth strip (H) parallel to (C). Weave it over (A), under (G), over (D), under (F), and over (B).

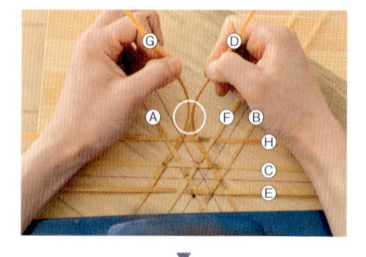

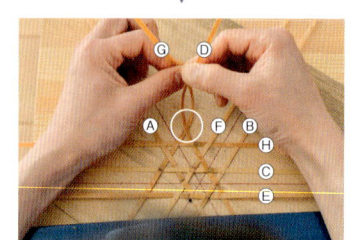

▼

⓭（D）と（G）を組み替える。

13. Rearrange strips (D) and (G).

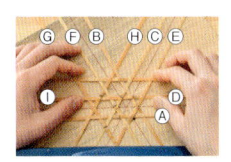

⓮左に60度回転し文鎮を置いて固定させる。9本目(Ⓘ)をⒹと平行におく。Ⓖをすくい、Ⓕをおさえ、Ⓗをすくい、Ⓑをおさえ、Ⓒをすくい、Ⓔをおさえる。

14. Rotate the weave 60° to the left and secure in place with the paperweight. Place the ninth strip (I) parallel to (D). Weave it under (G), over (F), under (H), over (B), under (C), and over (E).

⓯「左上がりのひごはおさえる」「右上がりのひごはすくう」「右端は常に上」「左端は常に下」の規則性で編み進む。
a:左上がりのひご
b:右上がりのひご

15. Continue weaving to the pattern of "over the upper-left strip", "under the upper-right strip", "right end is always on top", and "left end is always underneath".
a: The upper-left strips
b: The upper-right strips

⓰写真は12本目を編んだところ。右上がりのひご3本をすくい、左上がりのひご3本をおさえた状態になっている。このとき三角形の頂点が2つできるので、この2カ所のひごを組み替える。

16. The photograph shows the weave after the 12th strip. You can see that the horizontal strips go under the 3 upper-right strips, and over the 3 upper-left strips. Now you can form 2 peaks of a triangle, so rearrange the strips in 2 places.

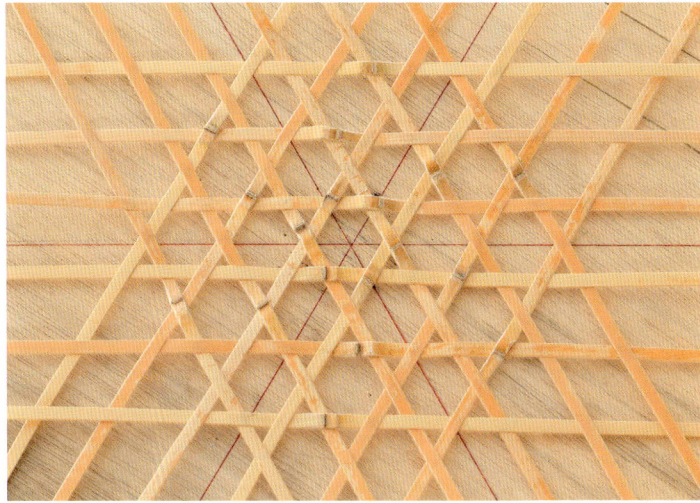

⓱六つ目編みで三段編んだもの。底編みが完成。

17. 3 levels woven with the mutsume weave. The base is now complete.

127

# STEP 2 ‣ 胴部分を編む
STEP 2: Weaving the trunk

⓱ 全体を霧吹きでしめらせて、竹ひごをやわらかくする。

18. Spray the entire weave with water to soften it up.

⓲ 身の方を上にして、六辺におこしぐせをつける。

19. Turn the weave over so the interior of the bamboo faces upwards, and put bends into the 6 groups of strips.

⓴ ひご作りのときにできた身竹を利用して仮力竹を3本作る。仮力竹は、おこす際に底を安定させるもの。材料は、ひご作りのときに余った身竹で作ることが多い。

20. Using the bamboo interior left over from when you made the bamboo strips, make 3 temporary bamboo reinforcement strips. These strips will help support the bottom when weaving upwards. They're usually made out of leftover bamboo interior.

㉑ 皮を外側にして、仮力竹を写真のように差し入れる。

21. Make it so the bark is on the outside and insert the supports as shown in the photograph.

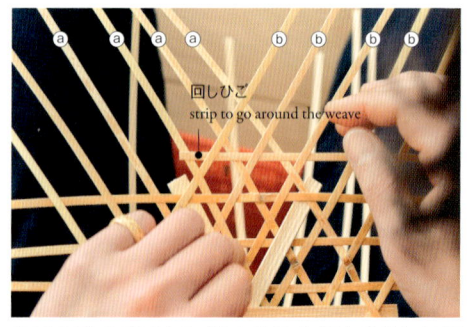

回しひご
strip to go around the weave

㉒ 1本の回しひごを入れる。「右上がりのひごはすくう」「左上がりのひごはおさえる」という規則性で編んでいく。
a: 左上がりのひご
b: 右上がりのひご

22. Insert one strip to go around the weave. Use the pattern "under the upper-right strips" and "over the upper-left strips".
a: Upper-left strips
b: Upper-right strips

㉓頂点を組み替える。

23. Rearrange the points of the triangles.

㉔角にきたら写真のように五角形にする。

24. When you come to a corner, make a pentagon as shown in the photograph.

㉕「6角形・6角形・5角形」の規則性で編み進んでいく。

25. Weave into a pattern of "hexagon → hexagon → pentagon".

㉖1周したらスタートのところをほどいて重ねる。

26. Once you've gone around the basket once, loosen the place where you started and slide the rest of the strip over it.

## STEP 2 ▸ 胴部分を編む  Weaving the trunk

㉗2段目は1段目と違うところからスタートする。1段目と同じように1本の回しひごを入れていく。

27. The 2nd level should be started from a different place to the first level. As with the first level, insert one strip to go all the way around.

㉘角の5角形のところにきたら5角形の上が「六つ目」の形になるように形を整える。

28. Adjust the shape so that the mutsume pattern appears above a pentagon at the corner.

㉙2段目が1周できたら、スタートをほどいて重ねる。3段目以降も、スタートは今までのところとずらして同様に編んでいく。

29. Once you've gone around once for the second level, loosen the start and lay the rest of the strip on top. From the third level onwards as well, shift the starting place each time and weave in the same way.

㉚5段の胴編みが完成。

30. The fifth level of the trunk is complete.

## STEP 3 ▶ 縁を編む

STEP 3: Weaving the rim

㉛右上がりのひご・左上がりのひごを、それぞれに編んでいく。

31. Weave each of the upper-right and upper-left strips.

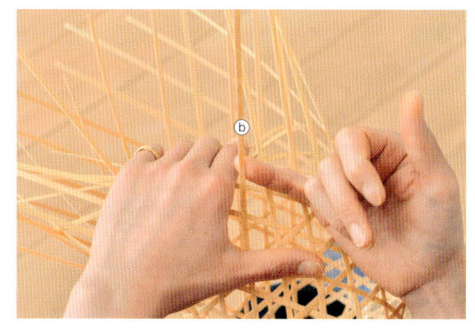

㉜最初は右上がりのひごから編んでいく。右上がりのひごの中から1本（ⓑ）を選ぶ。特に決まりはないので右上がりであればどれでもかまわない。

32. Start with the strips on the upper-right. From the strips on the upper-right, choose one (b). It doesn't particularly matter which one.

㉝右隣り2本のひごの下をくぐらせる。

33. Pass the strip under the 2 strips to its right.

㉞右隣り3本目・4本目の2本のひごをおさえる。

34. Pass it over the third and fourth strips to its right.

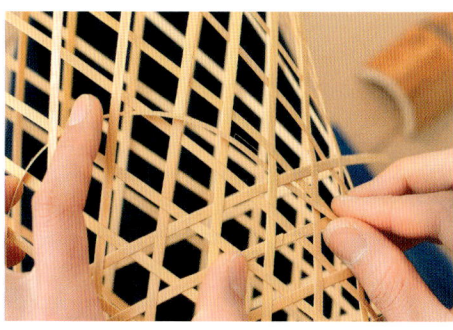

㉟写真の場所からひごを出す。

35. Push the strip out from the place in the photograph.

131

## STEP 3 ▶ 縁を編む  Weaving the rim

㊱ 隣に移動しながら、㉝、㉞、㉟の工程を繰り返していく。

36. While moving onto the next strip, repeat steps 33, 34, and 35.

㊲ 1周してきたら、スタートの1本目をゆるめて、その下をくぐらせる。

37. When you've gone around the basket once, loosen the first strip and pass the strip under.

㊳ 最後の1本は、スタートの1本目と2本目をゆるめて、その下をくぐらせる。

38. For the last strip, loosen the first two strips from the start and pass it through.

㊴ 左上がりのひごが残っている状態。

39. The upper-left strips remain.

㊵ 右上がりの工程と同様に、左上がりのひごの中から1本を選ぶ。右上がりとは反対周りで編んでいくので、選んだひごの左隣り2本の下をくぐらせる。

40. As with how you wove the upper-right strips, choose a strip from those on the upper-left. Weave them in the reverse direction to how you wove the upper-right strips, so weave the first strip under the two strips to the left.

132

㊶左隣り3本目、4本目、5本目の3本をおさえる。

41. Then weave it over the next three strips.

㊷写真の場所からひごを出す。㊵、㊶、㊷の工程を繰り返す。

42. Push the strip out from the place in the photograph. Repeat steps 40, 41, and 42.

㊸最後の1本はスタートの1本目と2本目をゆるめて、その下をくぐらせる。

43. Loosen the first two strips from the start and weave the last strip underneath.

Chapter 6

㊹余分なひごを剪定バサミでカットする。

44. Cut off any excess parts of the strip with pruning shears.

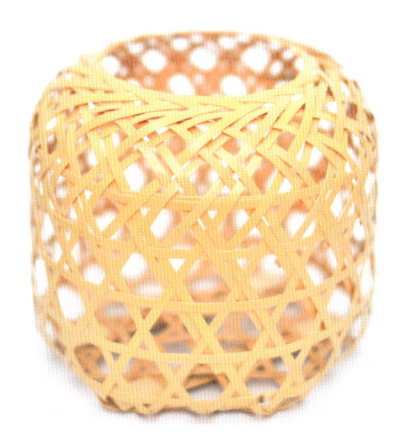

㊺縁が完成。

45. The rim is complete.

133

# STEP 4 ▸ 仕上げ ～力竹を入れる～

STEP 4: Finishing touches - inserting a support

㊻力竹のサイズはできあがったかごの底の大きさによるが、今回は幅15mm、厚み3mmの力竹を作る。まず、竹割り包丁で皮と身をわける。使うのは皮の部分なので、皮が3mmになるのが目安。

46. The size of the support strip will depend on the size of the base of the finished basket, but this time we will make a support that is 15mm wide and 3mm thick. Firstly, split the bamboo into bark and interior with a bamboo-cutting knife. The bark is what we're going to use, so aim to leave it about 3mm thick.

㊼竹割り包丁で面とりをする。

47. Cut away the sharpness of the sides with the bamboo-cutting knife.

㊽底の大きさに合わせてサイズを決める。

48. Decide on the size based on the size of the base.

㊾のこぎりで印を付けたところをカットする。

49. Use a saw to cut where you have marked.

㊿危ないし見た目もきれいではないので、竹割り包丁で角をとる。

50. Since they are dangerous and don't look very good, take off the corners with a bamboo-cutting knife.

(51)2本の力竹を入れて完成。

51. Insert the two support strips and it's done.

[ Chapter 6 ]

# お手入れ方法
Care methods

竹かごのお手入れ方法は、竹の種類で大きな違いはなく、湿気と直射日光に気をつけるところなどが共通しています。

The care of bamboo baskets doesn't greatly differ between the species. Paying attention to keeping the basket away from moisture and direct sunlight etc. is common across all types.

## 使うときに気をつけたいこと
Points to be aware of

1. 油が染み込むと落ちなくなる可能性があります。天ぷらなどの油を使った料理をのせるときは、クッキングシートなどを1枚しきましょう。その他、油分のあるお菓子などをのせるとき気になる場合も、写真のようにクッキングシートを使います。麺類やパンなどは、そのままのせて使う人が多いようです。

    If oil comes into contact with the bamboo, there is a possibility that it may not come out. When placing oily food such as tempura onto the bamboo, please line it with a sheet of baking paper or something similar beforehand. Put a sheet down like in the photograph for oily sweets as well if you feel that you need to. Many people put noodles or bread on the bamboo as-is.

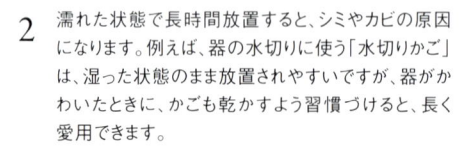

2. 濡れた状態で長時間放置すると、シミやカビの原因になります。例えば、器の水切りに使う「水切りかご」は、湿った状態のまま放置されやすいですが、器がかわいたときに、かごも乾かすよう習慣づけると、長く愛用できます。

    If you leave the bamboo damp for an extended period of time, it could cause discolouration or mould. Water draining baskets such as "mizukiri baskets" for example are easy to forget about when wet. By learning to make yourself dry the basket once the pots are dry, you can make the basket last far longer.

3. 変形や変色のおそれがあるので、食器洗浄機や電子レンジの使用は避けましょう。

    As there's a possibility that the baskets could get misshapen or discoloured, please refrain from putting them in the dishwasher or microwave.

## 毎日のお手入れ
Everyday care

1. 使用後は、手でやさしく水洗いします。汚れが気になるようなら、やわらかいスポンジに中性洗剤をつけ、編み目にそってやさしく洗います。
【注意ポイント】粗いスポンジやタワシなどで強くこすると、表面に傷がつく可能性がある。

After use wash the baskets carefully with water. If there are any stains that you would like to remove, try applying some neutral detergent to a soft sponge and washing the basket gently, following the direction of the stitching.
Caution: If you use a rough sponge or a scouring pad with some force, you risk damaging the surface of the bamboo.

2. 洗った後は、風通しのよいところで自然乾燥させます。湿気の多い日や早く乾かしたいときは、フキンなどで軽く水気を拭き取りましょう。
【注意ポイント】カビなどの原因になるので、濡れたまま湿気の多いところに放置しない。天日干しも避ける。

After washing, leave the basket to dry naturally in a well aired room. If the day is particularly humid, or you want the basket to dry faster, use a cloth to lightly wipe away any remaining moisture.
Caution: Please don't place the basket in humid places when wet, as this may cause mould to grow. Please also avoid drying in the sun.

3. 直射日光、湿度の高いところを避けて保管します。ざるなどは、洗った後にフックなどにかけておきましょう。

Please store the basket away from moisture and direct sunlight. For things like zaru plates, it's best to put them on hooks or something similar after washing.

### カビが生えてしまったら
If you find mould

拭いても取れないカビの場合、カビた部分にクレンザーをつけ歯ブラシでこすり、水で洗い流します。
【注意ポイント】クレンザーでこすると、カビといっしょに竹の表面が削れてしまう。その部分だけ色が変わってしまうことを、あらかじめ知っておこう。

If you find mould that cannot be wiped away with a cloth, try applying some cleanser to a toothbrush and rubbing the mouldy area, before rinsing with water.
Caution: If you brush at the mould with a cleanser, please understand that some parts of the surface of the bamboo may come away with the mould or it may result in a patch of discolouration.

# 作家リスト
Craftsmen directory

勢司恵美(せいし・えみ)
PROFILE／大学卒業後、沖縄でネイチャーガイドを経験したりと環境問題に関心を持ち、その観点から大分県竹工芸訓練支援センターで竹工芸を学ぶ。現在、故郷の茨城県行方市を拠点に「青物」を主とした竹工芸作家として活動。
【連絡先】emiseishi@hotmail.co.jp

内原聖次(うちはら・せいじ)
PROFILE／大学院修了後、電機メーカーにエンジニアとして就職。39歳で退職後、別府に移住し、大分県竹工芸訓練支援センターで竹工芸を学ぶ。現在は愛媛を拠点に竹工芸作家として活動しながら農業をいとなみ、自給自足の生活を実践している。
【連絡先】sy_uchi@plum.plala.or.jp

児玉美重(こだま・みえ)
「工房 東雲(しののめ)」
PROFILE／短大卒業後、財団法人に就職。退職後、大分県竹工芸訓練支援センターで竹工芸を学ぶ。2013年、アメリカのサンタフェ市で行われたTAI GALLERY竹アートコンペ「Emerging Bamboo」に『花籠 東雲(しののめ)』が入選。現在、大分県杵築市を拠点に活動中。
【連絡先】mie.sinonome@gmail.com

大谷健一(おおたに・けんいち)
「竹楓舎(ちくふうしゃ)」
PROFILE／大学卒業後、旅行会社などを経て、大分県竹工芸訓練支援センターで竹工芸を学ぶ。伝統工芸士・油布昌伯(ゆふ・まさたか)氏のもとで修業後、独立。別府を拠点に活動し、大分県竹産業文化連合会の中心メンバーでもあり、アメリカの「タイモダン」で展開する製品開発にも携わる。
【連絡先】taxus05@gmail.com

清水貴之(しみず・たかゆき)
PROFILE／大学時代、旅先の東南アジアで竹の魅力に触れたのをきっかけに竹工芸を志す。大学卒業後、大分県竹工芸訓練支援センターで竹工芸を学ぶ。伝統工芸士・森上智(もりがみ・さとし)氏のもとで修行し独立。拠点は別府だが、別府竹細工東京教室の講師も務めている。
【連絡先】takeyuki432@gmail.com

中岩考二(なかいわ・こうじ)
「竹工房かわせみ」
PROFILE／高校卒業後、現在の大分県竹工芸訓練支援センターで竹工芸を学ぶ。渡辺竹清(わたなべ・ちくせい)氏のもとで修業し独立。34歳の若さで伝統工芸士を取得。初代・太田龍々斎(おおた・りゅうりゅうさい)からの145年の伝統の技を受け継いでいる。別府を拠点に活動中。
【連絡先】sukupi@oct-net.ne.jp

岩田淳子(いわた・じゅんこ)
「工房 筍(たけのこ)」
PROFILE／大学卒業後、獣医師の仕事に就く。退職後、大分県竹工芸訓練支援センターで竹工芸を学ぶ。現在は大分県竹田市を拠点に、大好きな「角物」を中心で女性らしい視点を生かし、ヒット作品を作り出している。
【連絡先】koubou.takenoko@gmail.com

柴田恵(しばた・めぐみ)
PROFILE／高校卒業後、東京で会社勤務を経験。故郷の岩手県一戸に戻った後、本格的に「鳥越竹細工」に取り組む。2007年、「いわて特産品コンクール」で県知事賞受賞。

桑原哲次郎(くわばら・てつじろう)
「桑原竹細工店」
PROFILE／高校卒業後、広告会社でグラフィックデザイナーとして勤務。退職後、父のもとで竹細工を学ぶ。熊本県伝統的工芸品の指定を受けている「日奈久竹細工」の技を継承する、ただひとりの職人。
【連絡先】熊本県八代市日奈久中町315

井上栄一(いのうえ・えいいち)
「井上竹細工店」
PROFILE／高校卒業後、車のセールスなどに携わった後、20代後半で、根曲竹細工を志す。祖父、父から伝統の技を学ぶ。戸隠の根曲竹細工の数少ない継承者。
【連絡先】長野県長野市戸隠3416

取材協力
大崎市竹工芸館
【連絡先】〒989-6436
宮城県大崎市岩出山字二ノ構115

Emi Seishi
Profile: After graduating university, Seishi went on to become a nature guide in Okinawa and became interested in environmental issues. With that field of view, she went to learn bamboo crafts at the Oita Prefecture Bamboo Craft Training Support Center. She is currently living in her hometown of Namegata in Ibaraki Prefecture, where she is working as a bamboo craftsman who specializes in "Aomono".
Contact:emiseishi@hotmail.co.jp

Seiji Uchihara
Profile: After finishing graduate school, Uchihara worked as an engineer at an electrical manufacturer. After leaving at the age of 39, he moved to Beppu where he studied bamboo crafts at the Oita Prefecture Bamboo Craft Training Support Center. He currently works from Ehime as a bamboo craftsman while living a life of agriculture and self-sufficiency.
Contact: sy_uchi@plum.plala.or.jp

Mie Kodama
(Shinonome Studio)
Profile: After graduating junior college, she worked at a foundation. After leaving, she went to study bamboo crafts at the Oita Prefecture Bamboo Craft Training Support Center. In 2013, "Hanakago Shinonome" was chosen for the Tai Gallery's "Emerging Bamboo" bamboo art show in Santa Fe, USA. She currently works from Kitsuki, Oita Prefecture.
Contact: mie.sinonome@gmail.com

Kenichi Otani
(Chikufusha)
Profile: After graduating university, Otani spent some years working in a travel agency before going to study bamboo crafts at the Oita Prefecture Bamboo Craft Training Support Center. After studying under the traditional craftsman Masataka Yufu, he went independent. He works out of Beppu and is a key member of the Oita Prefecture Bamboo Industry & Culture Association. He's also associated with product development for the US "Taimodern".
Contact: taxus05@gmail.com

Takayuki Shimizu
Profile: During university Shimizu began to fall in love with the bamboo he saw on his travels to Southeast Asia, prompting him to aspire to be involved in bamboo crafts. After he graduated university he went to study bamboo crafts at the Oita Prefecture Bamboo Craft Training Support Center. He studied under the traditional craftsman Satoshi Morigami before becoming independent. Despite working mainly from Beppu, he also works at the Tokyo class of Beppu Bamboo Work.
Contact: takeyuki432@gmail.com

Koji Nakaiwa
(Kawasemi Bamboo Studio)
After graduating high school, Nakaiwa studied bamboo crafts at the current Oita Prefecture Bamboo Craft Training Support Center. He studied under Chikusei Watanabe before becoming independent. At just 34 years of age he acquired the traditional craftsman qualification and has been passed down a total of 145 years of traditional technique from the founder, Ryuryusai Ota. He currently works out of Beppu.
Contact: sukupi@oct-net.ne.jp

Junko Iwata
(Takenoko Studio)
Profile: After graduating university Iwata worked as a veterinarian. After leaving that job she went on to study bamboo crafts at the current Oita Prefecture Bamboo Craft Training Support Center. She currently works from Taketa, Oita Prefecture, where she makes hit "kakumono" products that make the most of her feminine vision.
Contact: koubou.takenoko@gmail.com

Megumi Shibata
Profile: After graduating high school, Shibata gained some experience working at a company in Tokyo. Upon returning to her hometown of Ichinohe, Iwate Prefecture, she decided to get to grips with authentic "Torigoe bamboo works". Won the Prefectural Governor Prize at the 2007 Iwate Special Product Contest.

Tetsujiro Kuwabara
(Kuwabara Bamboo Work Store)
Profile: After graduating high school, Kuwabara worked at an advertising company as a graphic designer. After leaving he began to study bamboo craft under his father. He is the only craftsman to inherit the "Hinagu bamboo work" techniques, which are designated as Kumamoto Prefecture traditional handicrafts.
Contact: 315 Hinagu nakamachi, Yatsushiro, Kumamoto Prefecture

Eiichi Inoue
(Inoue Bamboo Work Store)
Profile: After graduating high school, Inoue worked in car sales until he left to work with nemagaridake bamboo work in his late 20's. He learnt his techniques from his father and is one of few successors to the secrets of Togakushi nemagaridake bamboo works.
Contact: 3416 Togakushi, Nagano, Nagano Prefecture

Materials
Osaki Bamboo Crafts Hall
Contact: 115 Ninokamae Iwadeyama, Osaki, Miyagi Prefecture, 〒989-6436

# 取扱店リスト
Retailer's list

## 内原聖次

[縷縷]
オンラインショップ
http://www.luluweb.com
Lulu Shop at RANDY
〒106-0032 東京都港区六本木1-3-37
ARKHILLS ANNEX
[spica]
〒874-0939 大分県別府市立田町1-34
TEL 090-9476-0656
http://spica.tv/

## 児玉美重

[温温]
〒337-0001
埼玉県さいたま市見沼区丸ヶ崎1856
TEL 048-686-3620
[OUTBOUND]
〒180-0004
東京都武蔵野市吉祥寺本町2-7-4-101
TEL 0422-27-7720
[神楽坂 暮らす。]
〒162-0805 東京都新宿区矢来町68
アーバンステージ矢来101
TEL 03-3235-7758
[野の花 司]
〒104-0061 東京都中央区銀座3-7-21
TEL 03-3535-6929
[縷縷]
オンラインショップ
http://www.luluweb.com
Lulu Shop at RANDY
〒106-0032 東京都港区六本木1-3-37
ARKHILLS ANNEX
[ぎゃらりー 竹と和nagomi]
〒873-0001
大分県杵築市大字杵築338-1-1
TEL 070-6529-4663
[platform04 SELECT BEPPU]
〒874-0936 大分県別府市中央町9-33
TEL 0977-80-7226
[富士屋Galleryー也百(はなやもも)]
〒874-0046 大分県別府市鉄輪上1
TEL 0977-66-3251
FAX 0977-66-0302
http://www.fujiya-momo.jp

## 大谷健一

[世界のかご カゴアミドリ]
〒186-0004 東京都国立市中1-15-6
国立菅野ビル2F
TEL&FAX 042-507-9087
http://kagoami.com
[canna 家具店]
〒461-0012
愛知県名古屋市東区相生町14-1
http://cannakaguten.seesaa.net
TEL&FAX 052-933-6268
[竹かごどっとこむ]
http://www.takekago.com

## 中岩孝二

[竹細工の店 おかもと]
〒248-0034 神奈川県鎌倉市津西1-8-7
TEL 0467-31-9360
[工芸偕可園]
〒253-0056
神奈川県茅ヶ崎市共恵1-6-18
TEL 0467-85-7832
[サロン エスコ]
〒745-0031 山口県周南市銀南街15
TEL 0834-21-1729/0834-31-4129
FAX 0834-32-3250

## 清水貴之

[WISE.WISE tools]
〒107-0052 東京都港区赤坂9-7-4
東京ミッドタウン ガーデンサイド ガレリア
D-0313
TEL 03-5647-8355
FAX 03-5647-8356
http://www.wisewise.com/
[In-kyo]
〒111-0043 東京都台東区駒形2-5-1
TEL 03-3842-3577
http://www.in-kyo.net/
[Art+stellas 器物家(アステラスどうぐや)]
〒167-0051 東京都杉並区荻窪4-25-9
TEL 03-3393-4448
http://www.artstellasdoguya.com/

※この本に掲載された作家の作品を販売しているショップです。掲載作品が常備されていない場合もありますので、在庫状況につきましては、各店へご確認ください。※情報は2015年5月現在。
*These are the shops that sell the works of the craftsmen featured in this book. There may be cases when the product on display is not in stock, so please check stock levels with each shop. *Information up-to-date as of May 2015.

## Seiji Uchihara

[Lulu]
Online store: http://www.luluweb.com
Lulu Shop at Randy: 1-3-37 Arkhills Annex,
Roppongi, Minato-ku, Tokyo, 〒106-0032
[spica]
1-34 Tatsuta, Beppu, Oita Prefecture, 〒874-0939
TEL 090-9476-0656
http://spica.tv/

## Mie Kodama

[Nukunuku]
1856 Marugasaki, Minuma-ku, Saitama,
Saitama Prefecture, 〒337-0001
TEL 048-686-3620
[OUTBOUND]
101 2-7-4 Kichijoji Honmachi, Musashino, Tokyo,
〒180-0004
TEL 0422-27-7720
[Kagurazaka Kurasu.]
101 Urban Stage Yarai, 68 Yarai, Shinjuku-ku, Tokyo,
〒162-0805
TEL 03-3235-7758
[Nonohana Tsukasa]
3-7-21 Ginza, Chuo-ku, Tokyo, 〒104-0061
TEL 03-3535-6929
[Lulu]
Online store: http://www.luluweb.com
Lulu Shop at Randy: 1-3-37 Arkhills Annex,
Roppongi, Minato-ku, Tokyo, 〒106-0032
[Gallery Take to Wa Nagomi]
338-1-1 Kitsuki Oaza, Kitsuki, Oita Prefecture,
〒873-0001
TEL 070-6529-4663
[platform04 SELECT BEPPU]
9-23 Chuo, Beppu, Oita Prefecture, 〒874-0936
TEL 0977-80-7226
[Fujiya Gallery Hanayamomo]
1 Kannawa, Beppu, Oita Prefecture, 〒874-0046
TEL 0977-66-3251
FAX 0977-66-0302
http://www.fujiya-momo.jp

## Kenichi Otani

[Sekai no Kago: Kagoamidori]
Kokuritsu Kanno Building 2nd floor, 1-15-6 Naka,
 Kunitachi, Tokyo, 〒186-0004
TEL & FAX 042-507-9087
http://kagoami.com
[canna Furniture Store]
14-1 Aioi, Higashi-ku, Nagoya, Aichi Prefecture,
〒461-0012
http://cannakaguten.seesaa.net
TEL & FAX 052-933-6268
[takekago.com]
http://www.takekago.com

## Koji Nakaiwa

[Okamoto Bamboo Work Store]
1-8-7 Tsunishi, Kamakura, Kanagawa Prefecture,
〒248-0034
TEL 0467-31-9360
[Kaikaen Crafts]
1-6-18 Tomoe, Chigasaki, Kanagawa Prefecture,
〒253-0056
TEL 0467-85-7832
[Salon Esuko]
15 Ginnangai, Shunan, Yamaguchi Prefecture,
〒745-0031
TEL 0834-21-1729 / 0834-31-4129
FAX 0834-32-3250

## Takayuki Shimizu

[WISE. WISE tools]
D-0313 Tokyo Midtown Gardenside Galleria 9-7-4
Akasaka, Minato-ku, Tokyo, 〒107-0052
TEL 03-5647-8355
FAX 03-5647-8356
http://www.wisewise.com/
[In-kyo]
2-5-1 Komagata, Taito-ku, Tokyo, 〒111-0043
TEL 03-3842-3577
http://www.in-kyo.net/
[Art+stellag Asuterasdoguya]
4-25-9 Ogikubo, Suginami-ku, Tokyo, 〒167-0051
TEL 03-3393-4448
http://www.artstellasdoguya.com/

## 清水貴之

[世界のかご カゴアミドリ]
〒186-0004 東京都国立市中1-15-6
国立菅野ビル2F
TEL&FAX 042-507-9087
http://kagoami.com
[Ivory]
オンラインショップ http://www.ivory.jp/
[Hitofushi]
〒550-0003
大阪府大阪市西区京町堀1-12-28
壽会館ビル1階
TEL 06-6225-7675
http://hitofushi.com/
[ラボラトリオ]
〒390-0874 長野県松本市大手1-3-29
TEL 0263-36-8217
[hal]
〒410-0803 静岡県沼津市添地町124
TEL 055-963-2556
http://hal2003.net/
[cachito furniture]
〒651-1221 兵庫県神戸市北区緑町6-1-24
TEL 078-219-4592
http://www.cachitofurniture.com/
[tokineri]
〒812-0012
福岡県福岡市博多区博多駅中央街1-1
JR博多シティアミュプラザ博多7階
TEL 092-413-5338
http://www.tokineri.com/
[platform04 SELECT BEPPU]
〒874-0936 大分県別府市中央町9-33
TEL 0977-80-7226

## 岩田淳子

[縷縷]
オンラインショップ
http://www.luluweb.com
Lulu Shop at RANDY
〒106-0032 東京都港区六本木1-3-37
ARKHILLS ANNEX
[ギャラリー元浜]
〒500-8028 岐阜県岐阜市西材木町41-2
ナガラガワフレーバー 内
TEL 058-263-1227
http://www.n-flavor.net/motohama/
[暮らしの日用雑貨店 inthefield]
〒509-0237 岐阜県可児市桂ヶ丘1-155
TEL&FAX 0574-64-4633
http://inthe-field.shop-pro.jp/

[楓うつわ・珈琲]
〒762-0085
香川県丸亀市飯山町東小川西1252-1
TEL&FAX 0877-85-8023
[さかな]
〒491-0858 愛知県一宮市栄4-7-14
TEL 0586-72-3755
[ツバメ舎]
〒443-0047
愛知県蒲郡市西迫町馬乗70-1
TEL 0533-65-9973
http://tsubame-sha.com/
[SOKOYA]
〒631-0062 奈良県奈良市帝塚山3-21-19
TEL 0742-46-6136
http://sukoya.info/
[富士屋Gallery一也百(はなやもも)]
〒874-0046 大分県別府市鉄輪上1
TEL 0977-66-3251
FAX 0977-66-0302
http://www.fujiya-momo.jp

## 柴田恵

[暮らしのクラフトゆずりは]
〒018-5501
青森県十和田市大字
奥瀬字十和田湖畔休屋486
TEL 0176-75-2290
FAX 0176-75-2295
http://www.yuzuriha.jp/
[光原社]
〒020-0063 岩手県盛岡市材木町2-18
TEL 019-622-2894
FAX 019-622-2892
[ひめくり]
〒020-0885 岩手県盛岡市紺屋町4-8
TEL&FAX 019-681-7475

## 桑原哲次郎

[桑原竹細工店]
〒869-5135 熊本県八代市日奈久中町315
TEL 0965-38-2621

## 井上栄一

[井上竹細工店]
〒381-4101 長野県長野市戸隠3416
TEL 026-254-2181

## Takayuki Shimizu

[Sekai no Kago: Kagoamidori]
Kokuritsu Kanno Building 2nd floor, 1-15-6 Naka,
Kunitachi, Tokyo, 〒186-0004
TEL & FAX 042-507-9087
http://kagoami.com
[Ivory]
Online store: http://www.ivory.jp/
[Hitofushi]
1st floor Kotobuki Kaikan, 1-12-28 Kyomachibori,
Nishi-ku, Osaka, Osaka, 〒550-0003
TEL 06-6225-7675
http://hitofushi.com/
[Raboratorio]
1-3-29 Ote, Matsumoto, Nagano Prefecture,
〒390-0874
TEL 0263-36-8217
[hal]
124 Soechicho, Numazu, Shizuoka Prefecture,
〒410-0803
TEL 055-963-2556
http://hal2003.net/
[cachito furniture]
6-1-24 Midorimachi, Kita-ku, Kobe,
Hoygo Prefecture, 〒651-1221
TEL 078-219-4592
http://www.cachitofurniture.com/
[tokineri]
7th floor JR Hakata City AmuPlaza Hakata
1-1 Hakata Station Chuogai, Hakata-ku, Fukuoka,
Fukuoka Prefecture, 〒812-0012
TEL 092-413-5338
http://www.tokineri.com/
[platform04 SELECT BEPPU]
9-23 Chuo, Beppu, Oita Prefecture, 〒874-0936
TEL 0977-80-7226

## Junko Iwata

[Lulu]
Online store: http://www.luluweb.com
Lulu Shop at Randy: 1-3-37 Arkhills Annex,
Roppongi, Minato-ku, Tokyo, 〒106-0032
[Gallery Motohama]
Inside Nagaragawa Flavor, 41-2 Nishizaimokucho,
Gifu, Gifu Prefecture, 〒500-8028
TEL 058-263-1227
http://www.n-flavor.net/motohama/
[Daily Sundried inthefield]
1-155 Katsuragaoka, Kani, Gifu Prefecture,
〒509-0237
TEL & FAX 0574-64-4633
http://inthe-field.shop-pro.jp/

[Kaede Utsuwa / Coffee]
1252-1 West Higashi Ogawa, Hanzancho,
Marugame, Kagawa Prefecture, 〒762-0085
TEL & FAX 0877-85-8023
[Sakana]
4-7-14 Sakae, Ichinomiya, Aichi Prefecture,
〒491-0858
TEL 0586-72-3755
[Tsubame Sha]
70-1 Nishihasamacho Manori, Gamagori,
Aichi Prefecture, 〒443-0047
TEL 0533-65-9973
http://tsubame-sha.com/
[SOKOYA]
3-21-19 Tezukayama, Nara, Nara Prefecture,
〒631-0062
TEL 0742-46-6136
http://sukoya.info/
[Fujiya Gallery Hanayamomo]
1 Kannawa, Beppu, Oita Prefecture, 〒874-0046
TEL 0977-66-3251
FAX 0977-66-0302
http://www.fujiya-momo.jp

## Megumi Shibata

[Kurashi no Craft Yuzuriha]
486 Towadakohanayasumiya-Okuse, Towada,
Aomori Prefecture, 〒018-5501
TEL 0176-75-2290
FAX 0176-75-2295
http://www.yuzuriha.jp/
[Kogensha]
2-18 Zaimokucho, Morioka, Iwate Prefecture,
〒020-0063
TEL 019-622-2894
FAX 019-622-2892
[Himekuri]
4-8 Konyacho, Morioka, Iwate Prefecture,
〒020-0885
TEL & FAX 019-681-7475

## Tetsujiro Kuwabara

[Kuwabara Bamboo Works Store]
315 Hinagu-Nakamachi, Yatsushiro,
Kumamoto Prefecture, 〒869-5135
TEL 0965-38-2621

## Eiichi Inoue

[Inoue Bamboo Works Store]
3416 Togakushi, Nagano, Nagano Prefecture,
〒381-4101
TEL 026-254-2181

編集・執筆　嶋崎千秋　Editor / Write: Chiaki Shimazaki
撮影　臼田尚史　Photo: Naoshi Usuda
デザイン　佐藤アキラ　Design: Akira Sato
翻訳　カーリー・レッドフォールド　Translator: Carley Radford

Japanese-English Bilingual Books

英語訳付き

# 竹かごハンドブック
The Bamboo Basket Handbook

竹かごの素材、種類、選び方から、編み方、メンテナンスまでわかる

2015年6月15日　発　行　　　　　　　　　NDC 790

編　者　竹かご部
発行者　小川雄一
発行所　株式会社 誠文堂新光社
　　　　〒113-0033 東京都文京区本郷3-3-11
　　　　（編集）電話 03-5805-7285
　　　　（販売）電話 03-5800-5780
　　　　http://www.seibundo-shinkosha.net/

印刷所　株式会社 大熊整美堂
製本所　和光堂 株式会社

©2015, Seibundo Shinkosha Publishing Co.,Ltd.
Printed in Japan

検印省略　禁・無断転載

落丁・乱丁本はお取り替え致します。

本書のコピー、スキャン、デジタル化等の無断複製は、著作権法上での例外を除き、禁じられています。本書を代行業者等の第三者に依頼してスキャンやデジタル化することは、たとえ個人や家庭内での利用であっても著作権法上認められません。

R〈日本複製権センター委託出版物〉本書を無断で複写複製（コピー）することは、著作権法上での例外を除き禁じられています。本書をコピーされる場合は、事前に日本複製権センター（JRRC）の許諾を受けてください。
JRRC〈http://www.jrrc.or.jp/　E-mail:jrrc_info@jrrc.or.jp
電話03-3401-2382〉

ISBN978-4-416-71547-5